Landscapes and Wildlife

Artistic Impressions

By Craig Michael Maki

Published in

THE UNITED STATES OF AMERICA

© 2019 by Craig Michael Maki

Copyright Registered with the Library of Congress
First American Edition

Protected under the Copyright Laws of the
United States of America.
Protected under the Copyright Laws of Canada
All Worldwide Rights Reserved

Everett Source Publishing

"Varying landscapes have always been a favorite subject of my artistic creations. Yet sometimes I love to focus on the details found within those beautiful landscapes. I sincerely hope you enjoy them as much as I do."

Craig Maki

I dedicate this book to my loving family.

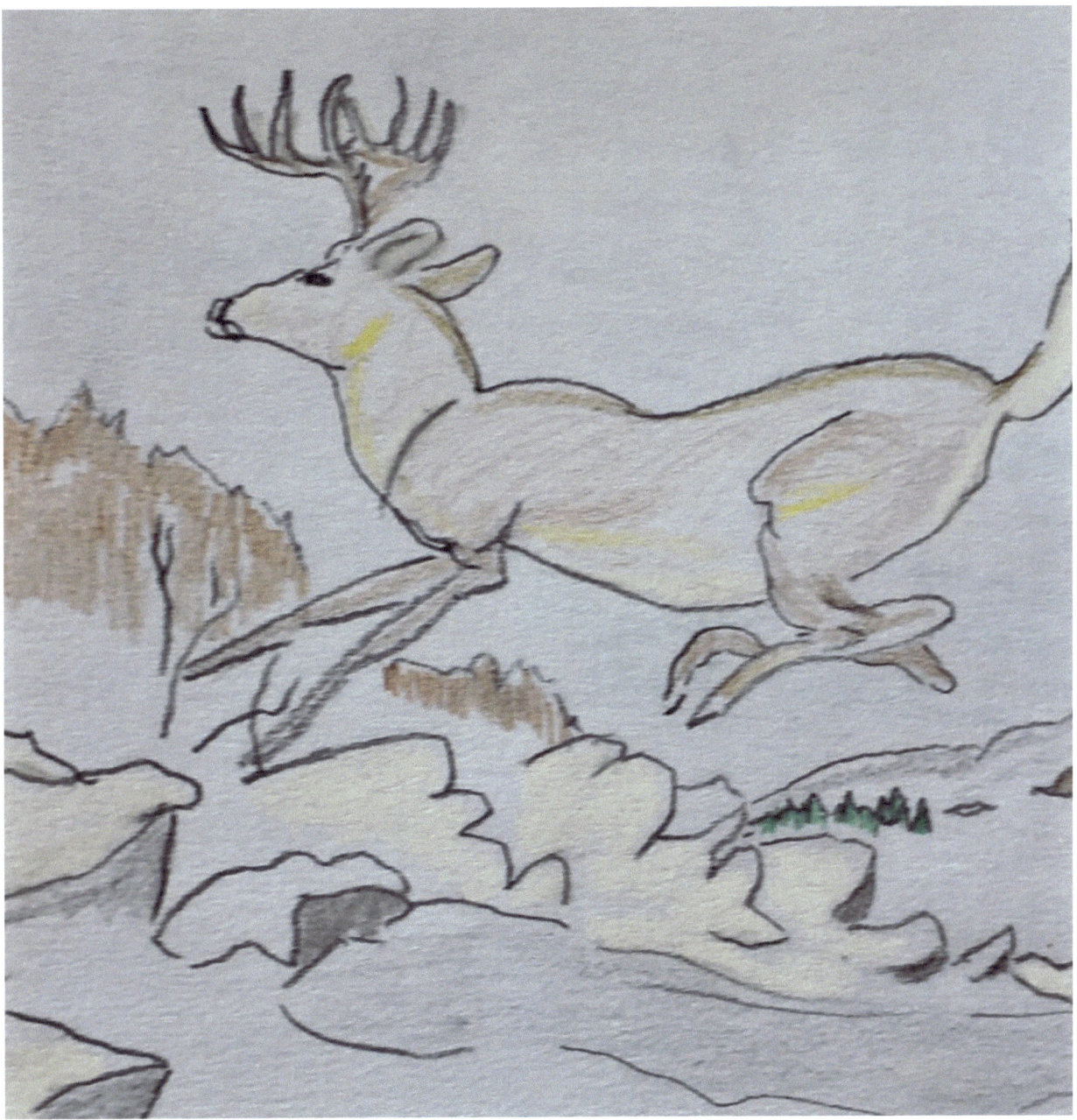

Whitetail Buck Deer © 2019 by Craig Michael Maki

"To me, nothing has the grace and stamina of a prancing Whitetail buck deer as it effortlessly bounds across the rugged terrain."

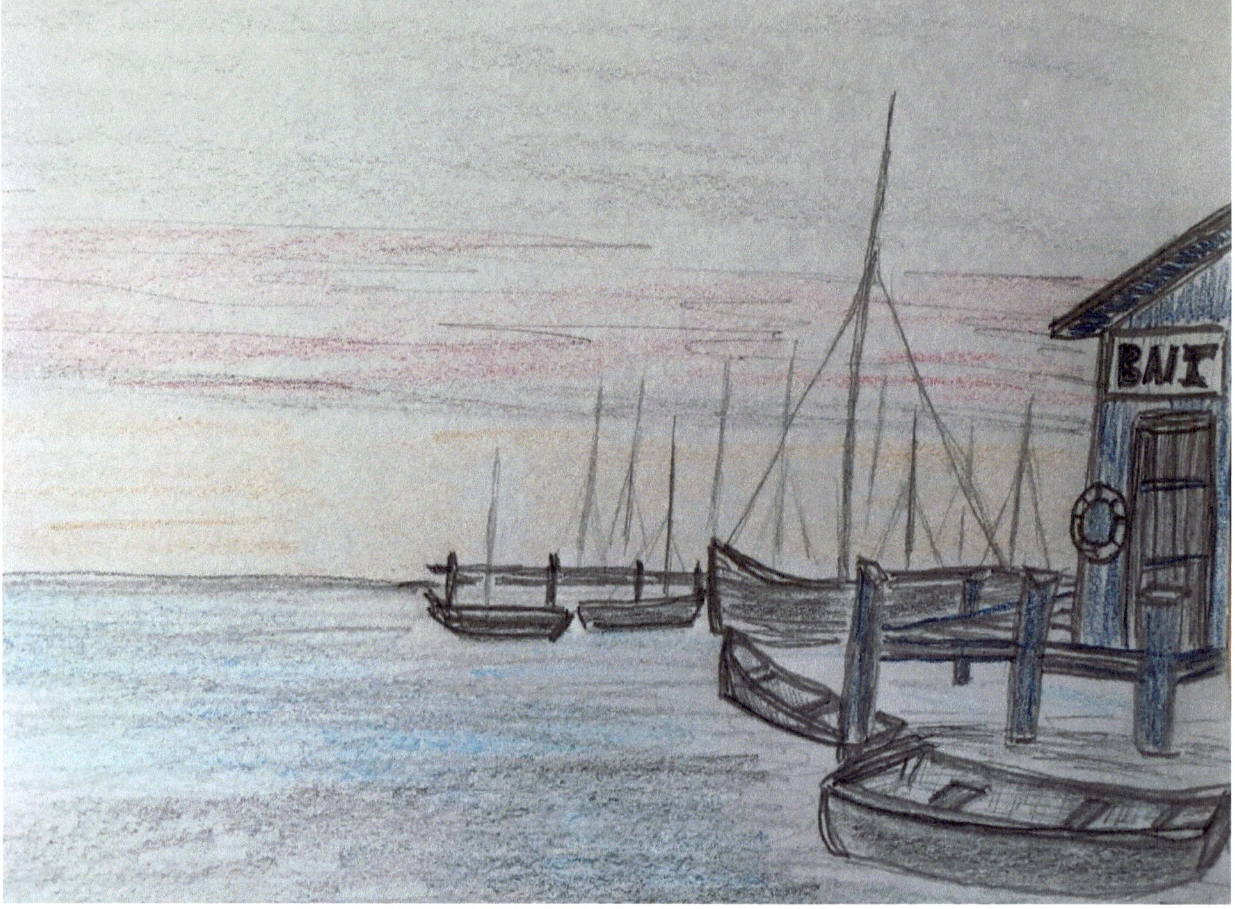

The Bait Dock   © 2019 by Craig Michael Maki

"I've always enjoyed a peaceful sunset over a quaint little fishing marina."

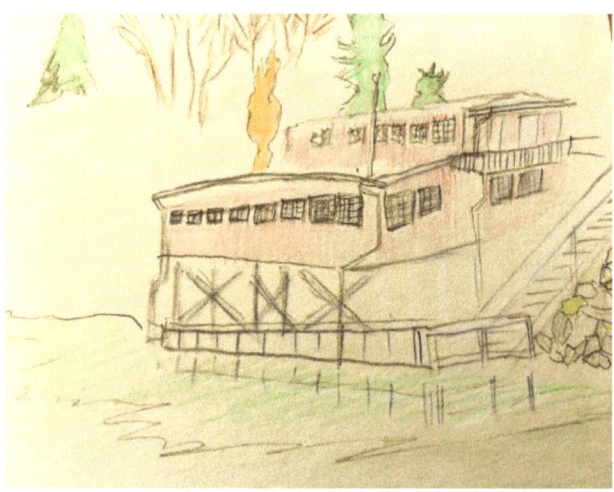

"Friday Harbor is a peaceful little town nestled in a picturesque harbor on San Juan Island. You get there by a ferry boat that zig-zags between numerous islands located in a mild climate that is restful and comfortable."

Friday Harbor, WA
© 2019 by Craig Michael Maki

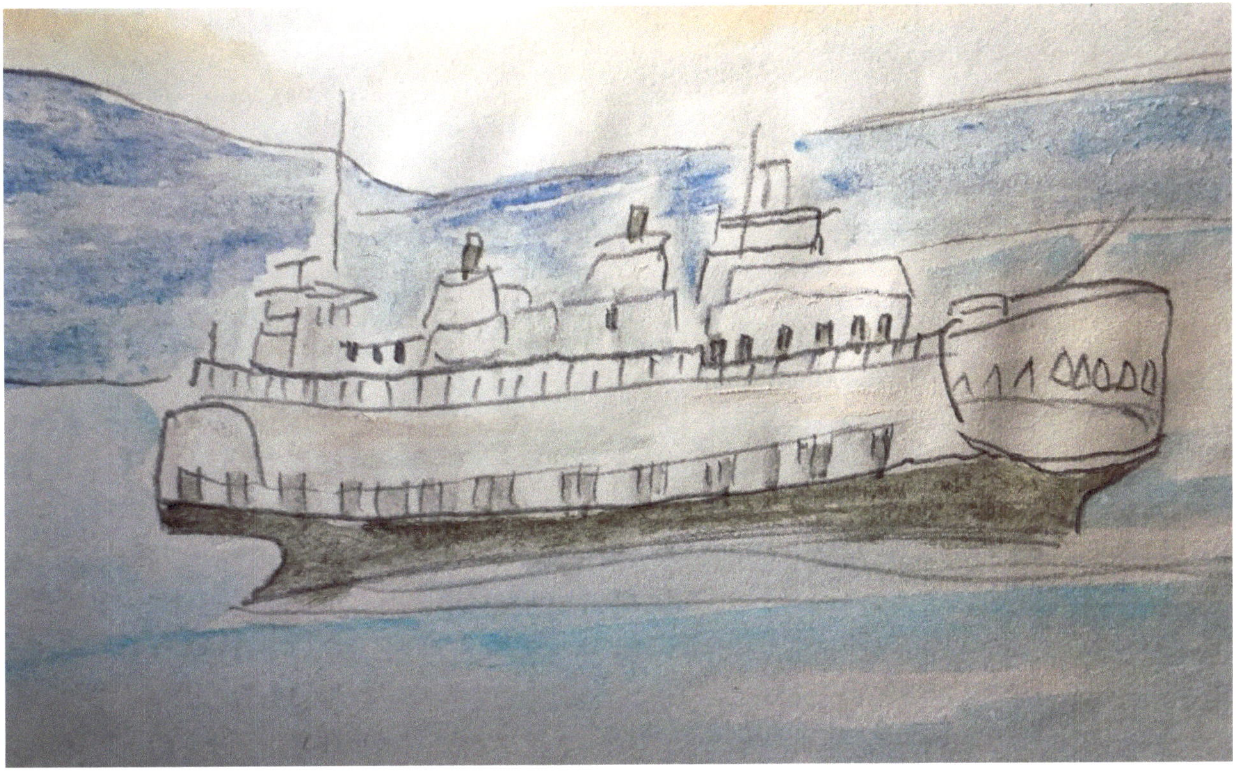

Ferry in the San Juan Islands © 2019 by Craig Michael Maki

"The marine ferry system in Washington State offers a unique experience to travel the inland passageways of the Puget Sound Region, while gazing at the unequaled beauty of the Pacific Northwest."

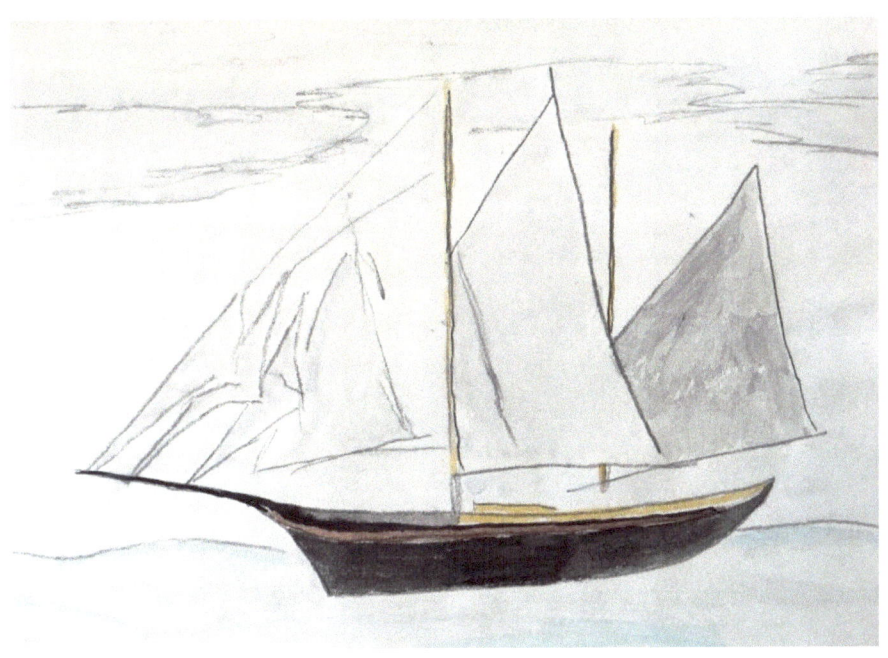

"The wind-filled sails of a sleek sailing schooner provide a clean efficient forward glide through inky blue waters."

Sailing Schooner
© 2019 by
Craig Michael Maki

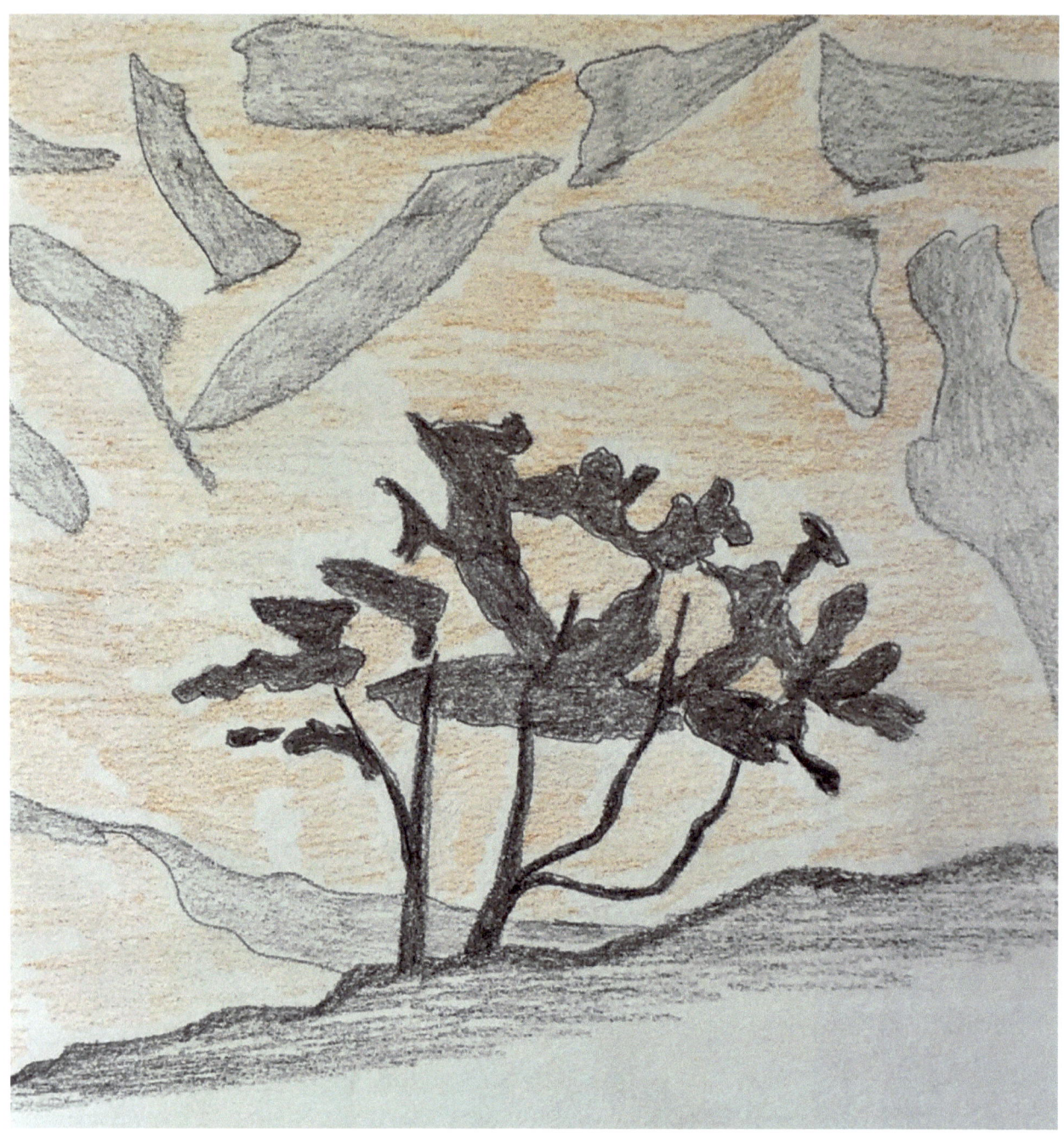

Sunset Silhouette © 2019 by Craig Michael Maki

"I have always loved to view a sturdy old tree on a ridge crest – silhouetted against the orange skies of a gorgeous sunset."

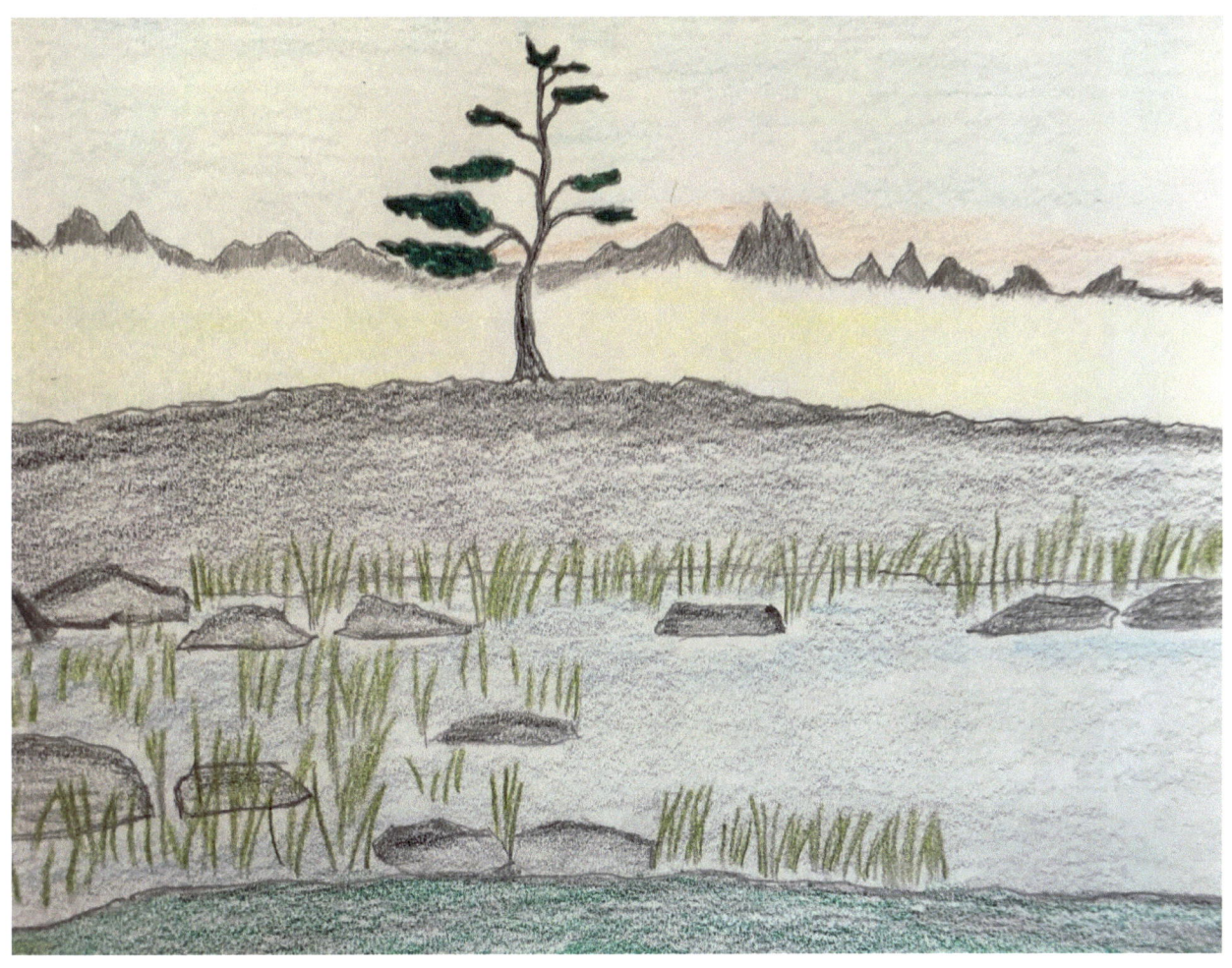

Ancient Monarch of the High Country © 2019 by Craig Michael Maki

"I was recently hiking along the alpine slopes of Mt. Baker, WA when I came upon a 700 year old pine tree that stood a timeless watch over a delicate lake.

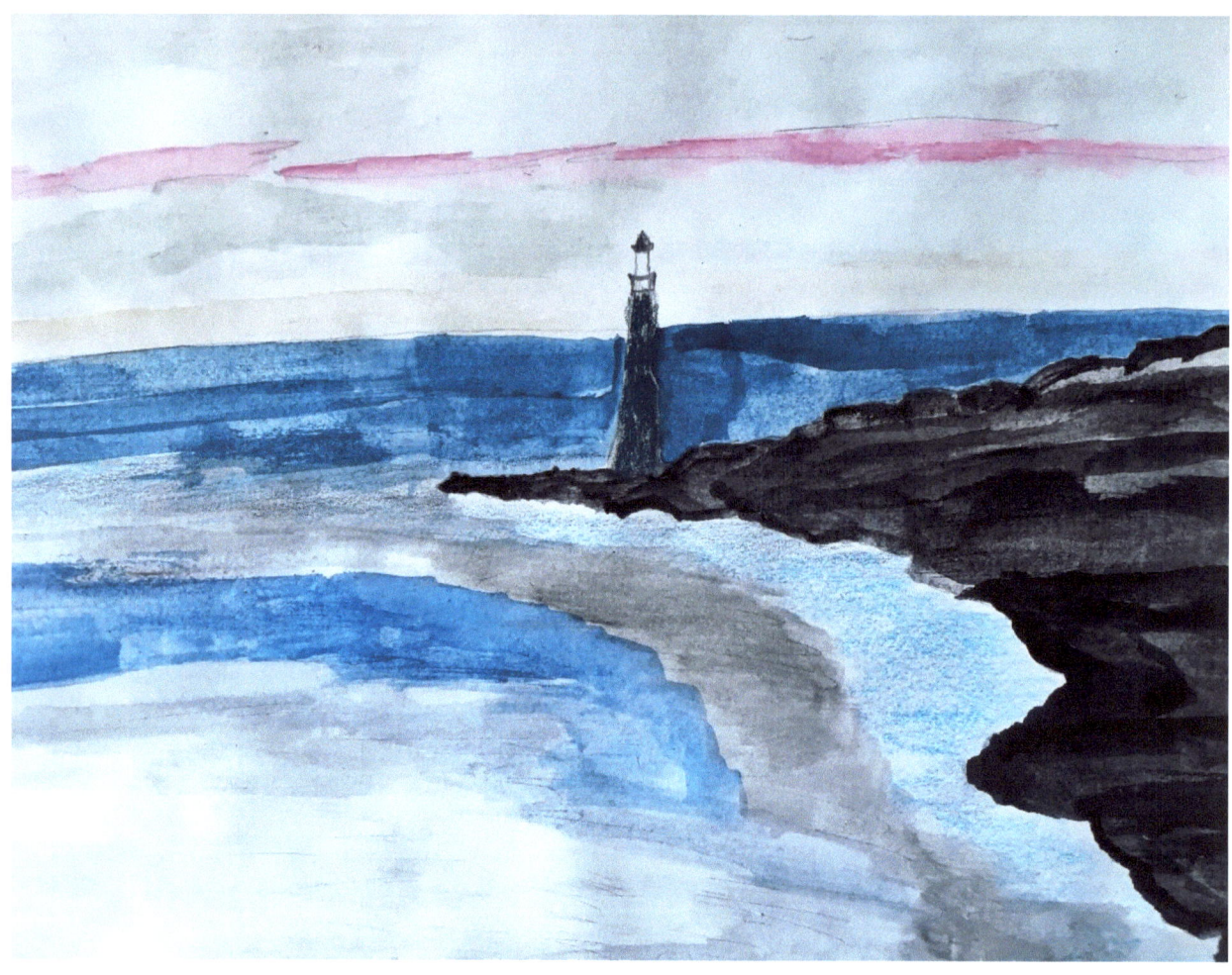

Sentinel of the Sea © 2019 by Craig Michael Maki

"Lighthouses have always fascinated me and I love to paint and draw them. Providing guidance away from rocky shores, a lighthouse always shows the way to safe harbors."

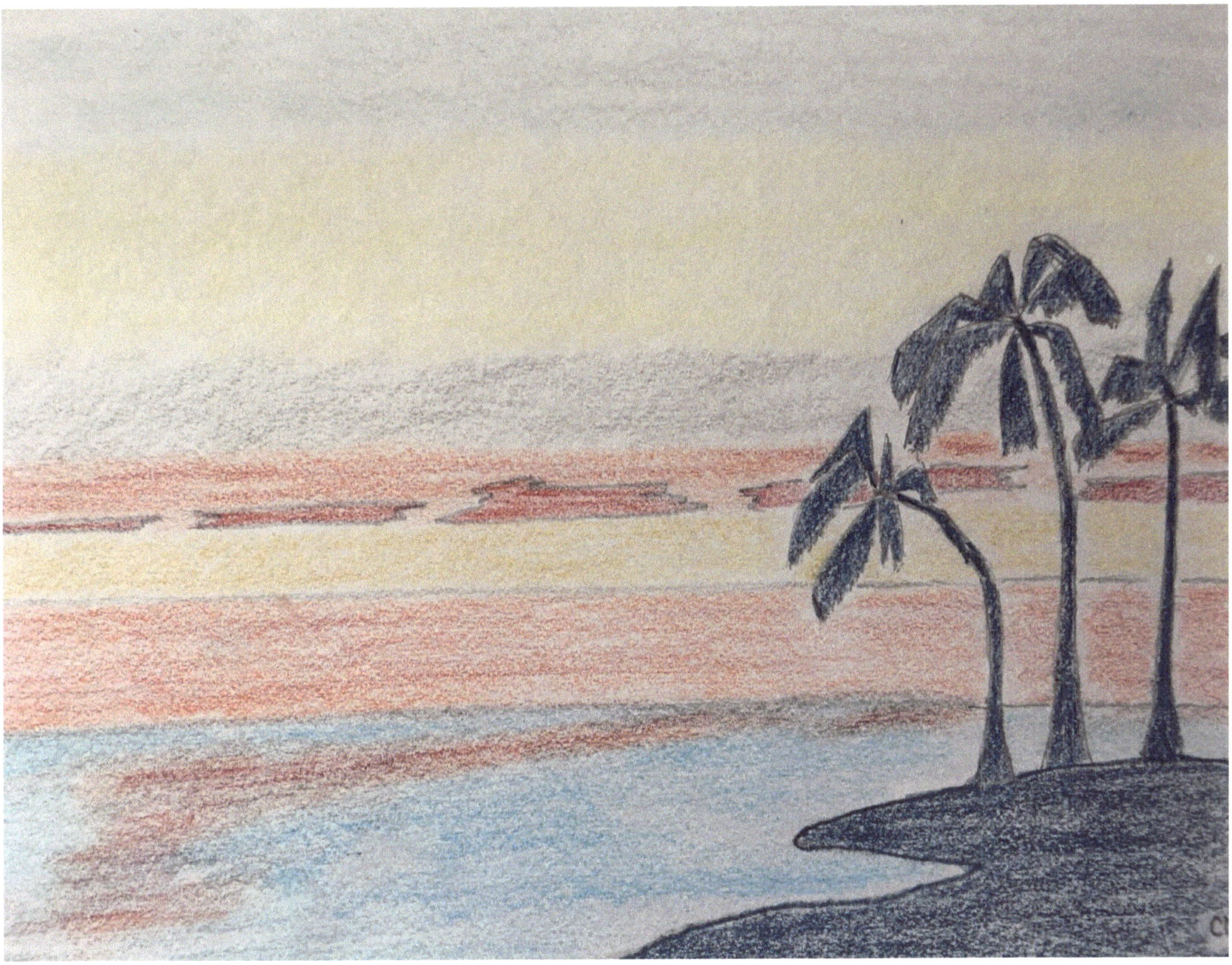

Tropical Paradise © 2019 by Craig Michael Maki

"Nothing tops a tropical sunset that casts its colorful rays across a palm tree laden shoreline."

"The tropics are so unique and the colors they release at sunset are tranquil and healing."

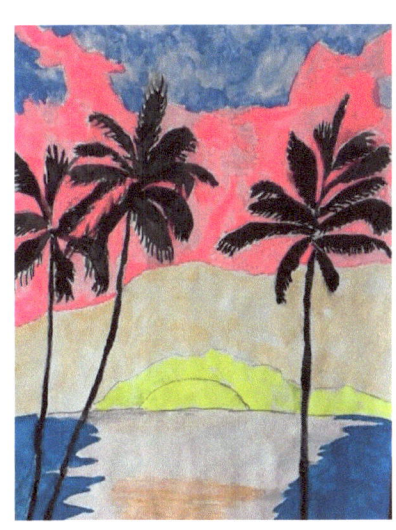

Triple Palm Sunset
© 2019 by Craig Michael Maki

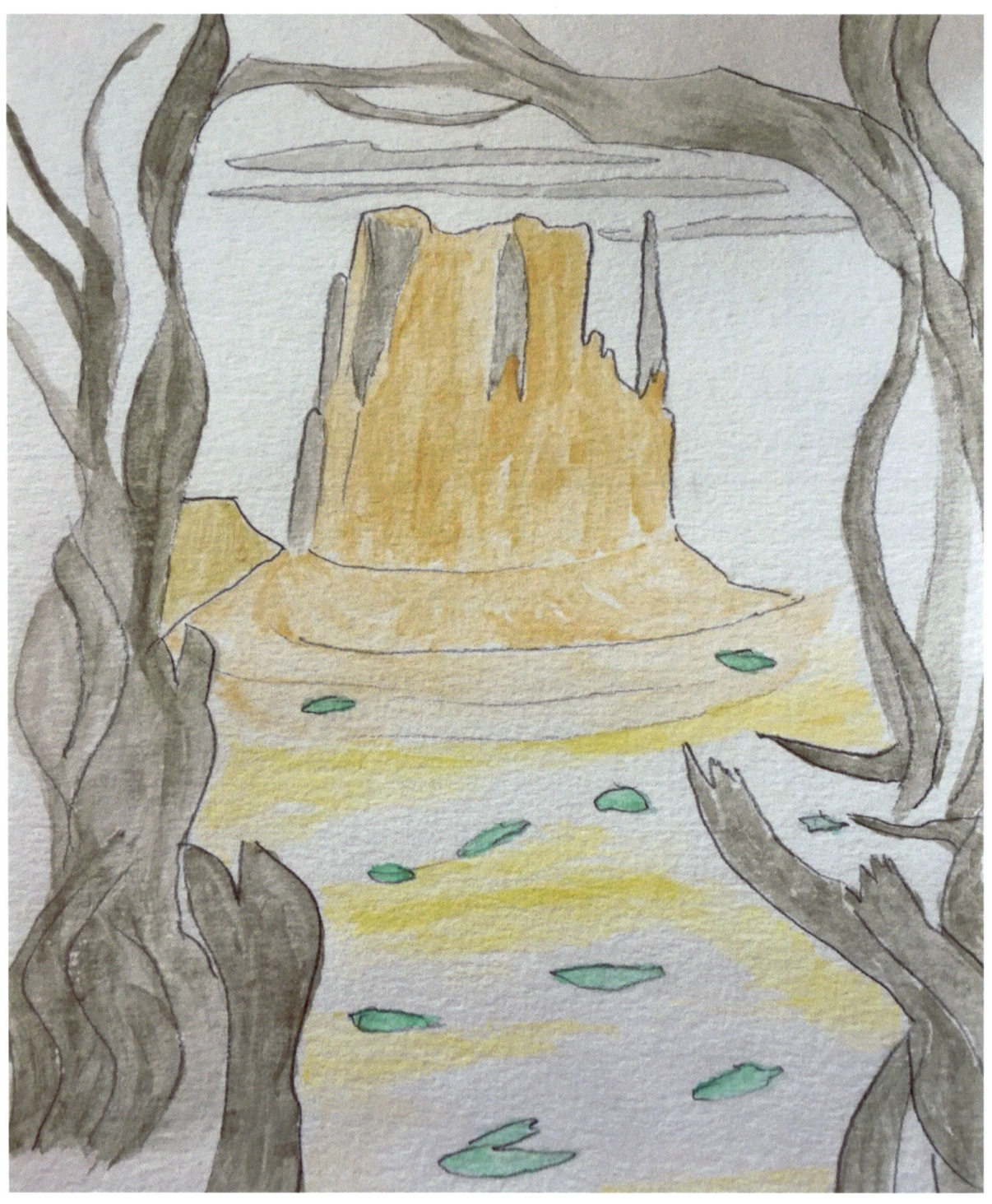

Monument Valley © 2019 by Craig Michael Maki

"These sandstone monoliths stand the test of time."

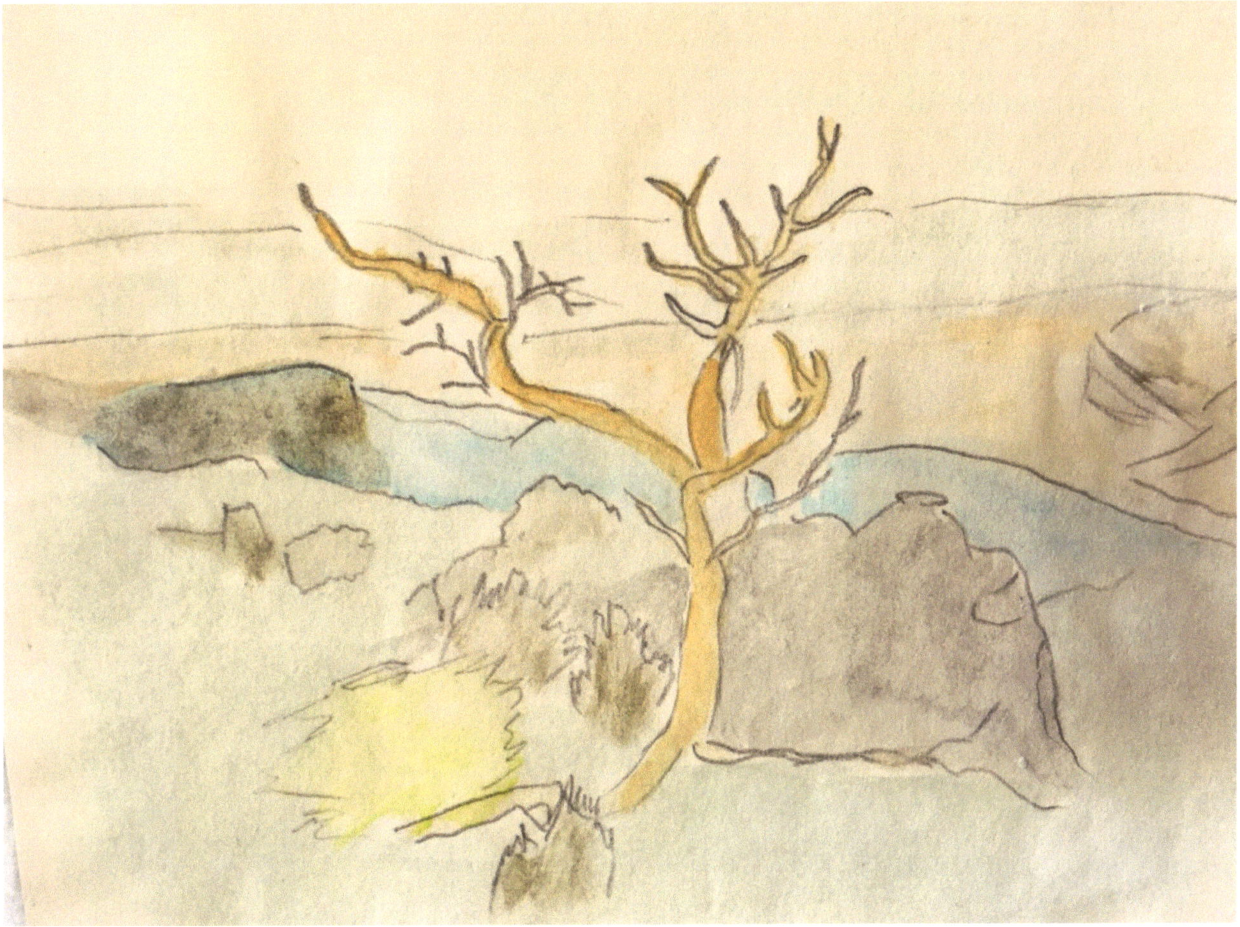

Missouri River Vista © 2019 by Craig Michael Maki

"Over two centuries ago Lewis and Clark traveled up the Missouri River to explore the American West, and they passed scenic terrain much like this."

"Pioneers bravely survived the elements in these handcrafted structures – some still stand today."

Pioneer Cabin
© 2019 by Craig Michael Maki

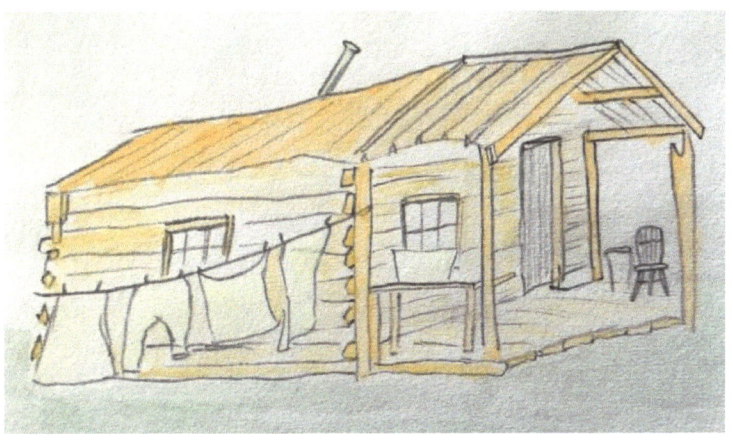

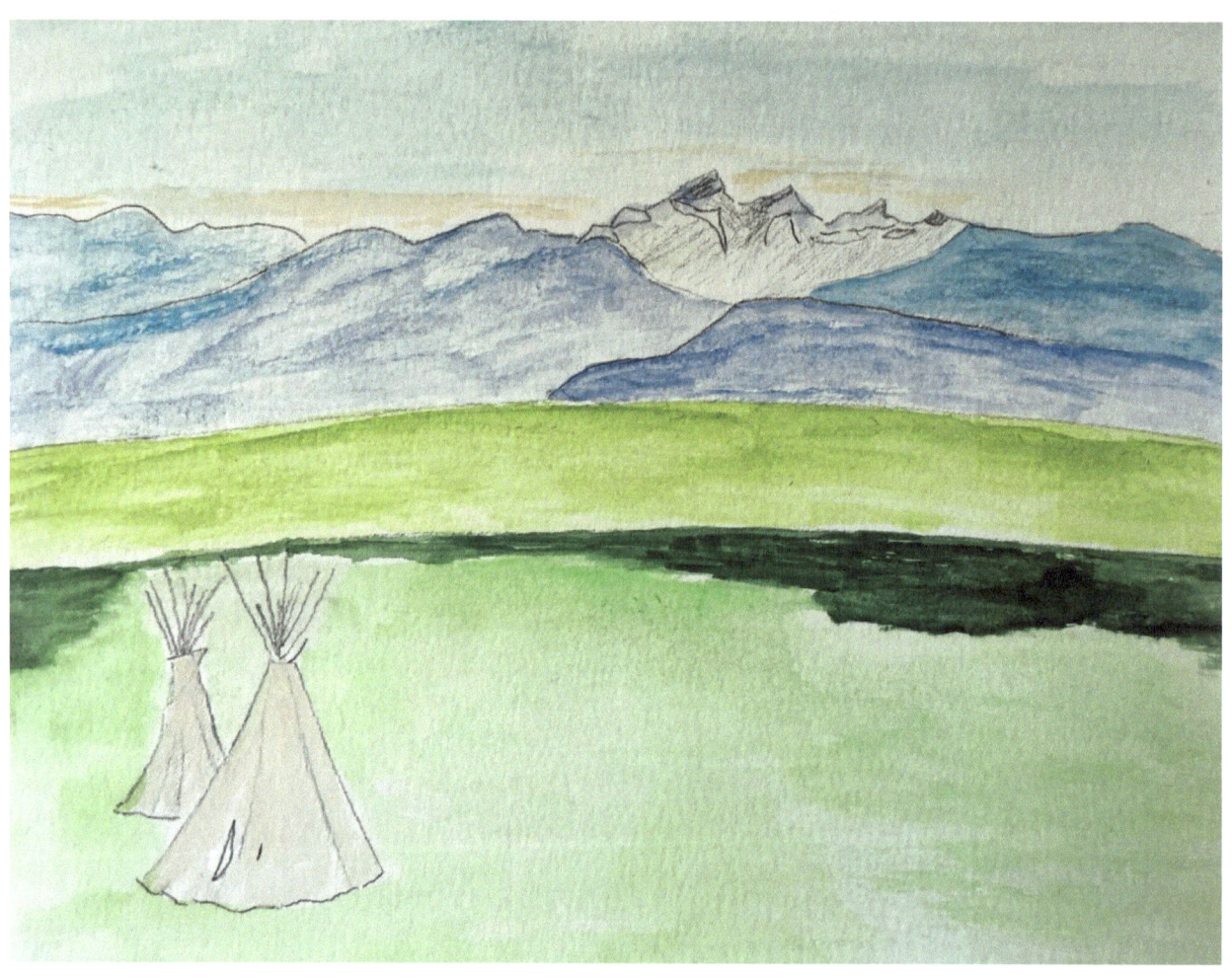

Twin Teepees in the Bitteroot Valley © 2019 by Craig Michael Maki

"Over two centuries have passed since Lewis and Clark descended into the Bitteroot Valley – to be met by hundreds of Native Americans who lent food, horses and route knowledge to the expedition leaders."

"Peace can always be found in the mountains."

High Country Solitude
© 2019 by Craig Michael Maki

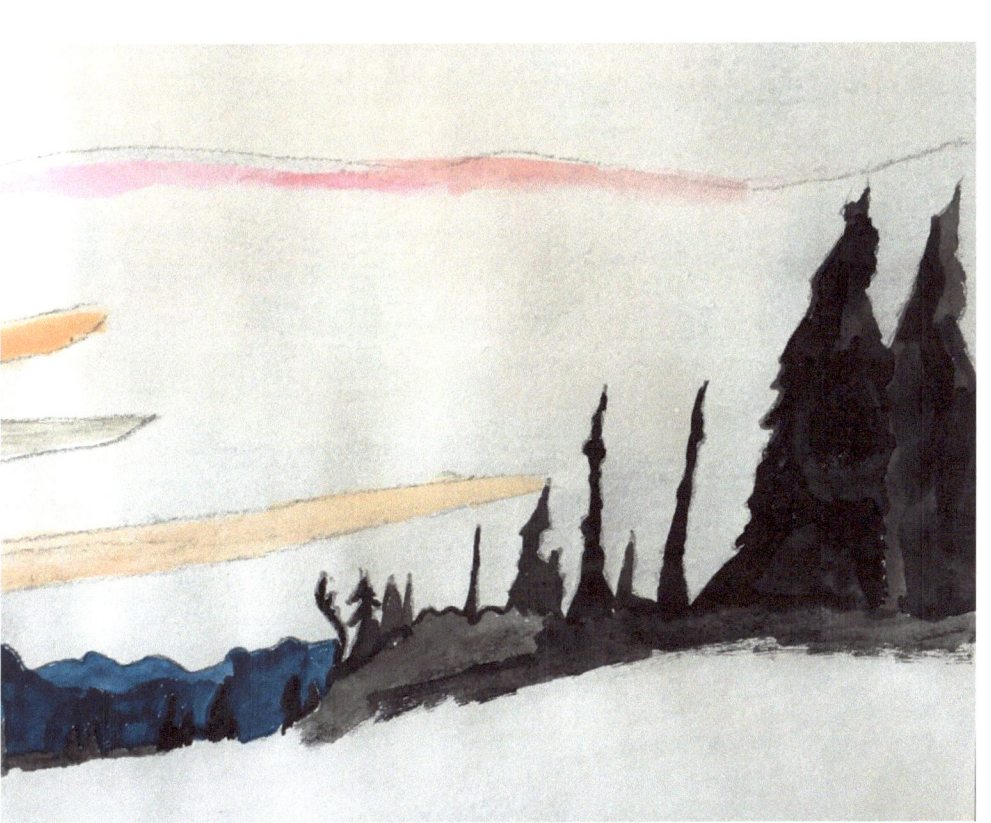

"There is absolutely nothing like the fresh scent of ionized oxygenated mountain air."

Crisp Mountain Air

© 2019 by Craig Michael Maki

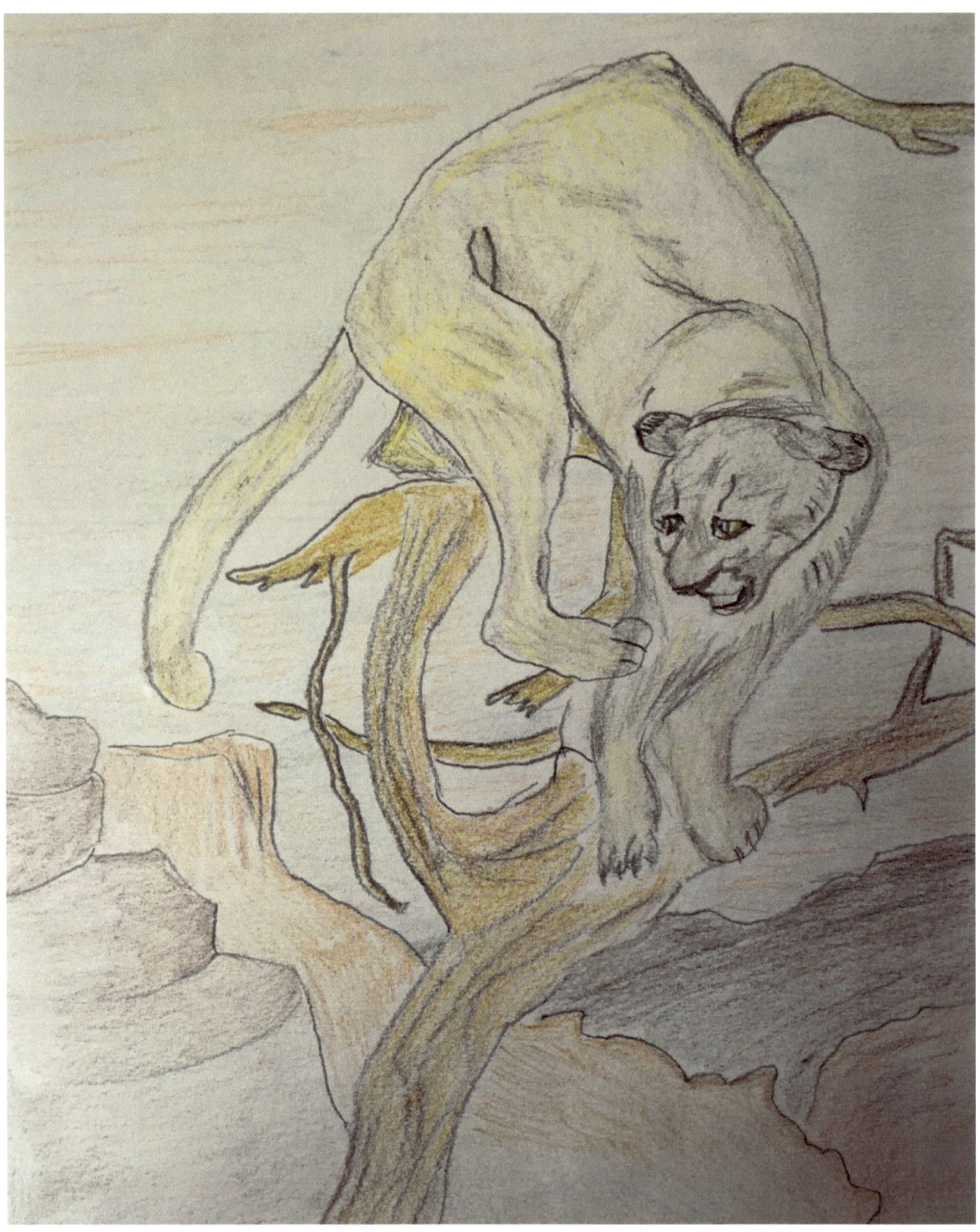

Lion of the Mountains © 2019 by Craig Michael Maki

"I have always been extra aware when hiking in Mountain Lion country – always looking upward."

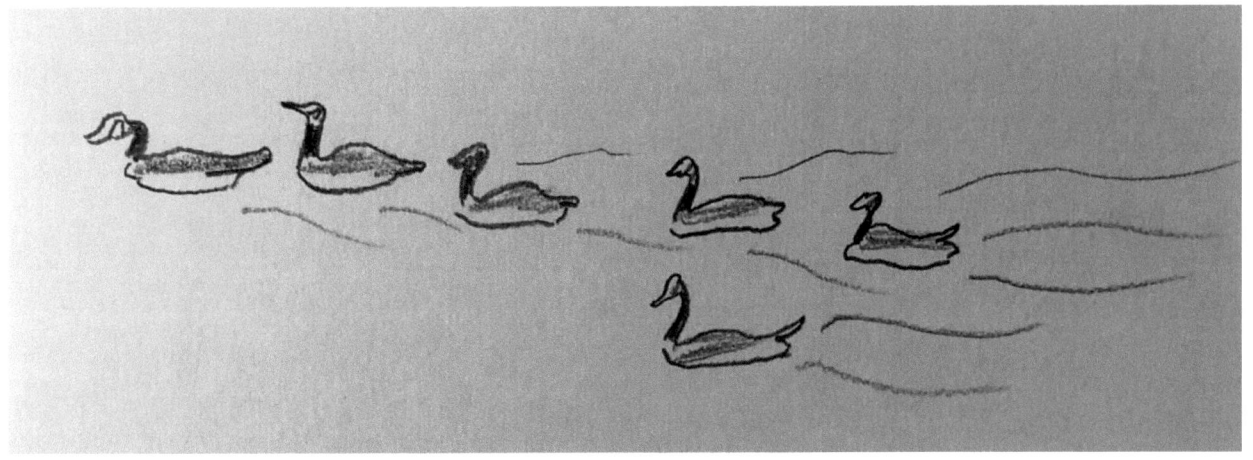

Canadian Honkers © 2019 by Craig Michael Maki

"There is nothing like the sound of a flock of Canadian Geese flying in formation overhead, and nothing more quiet than these same Canadian Honkers gently swimming on a calm lake."

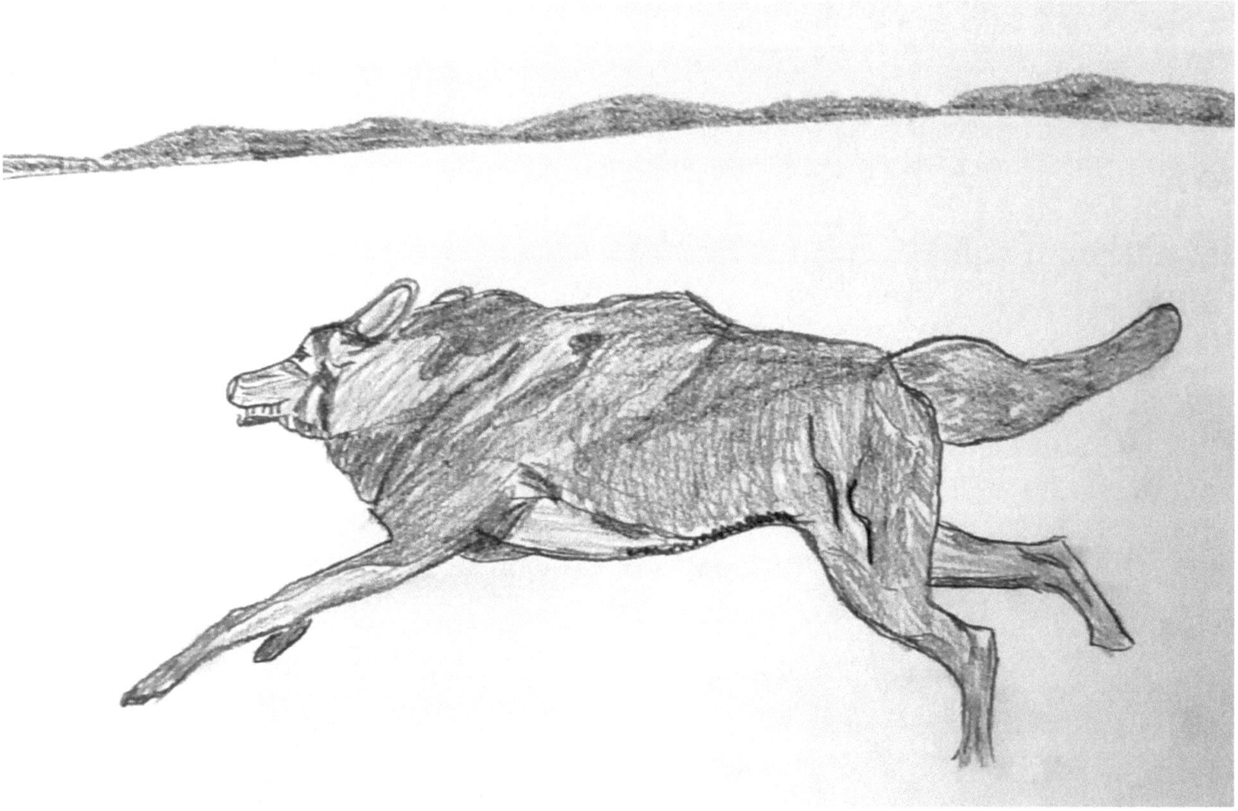

Wolf © 2019 by Craig Michael Maki

"I never forget the thrill of seeing a wolf bound across a meadow in Grand Teton National Park."

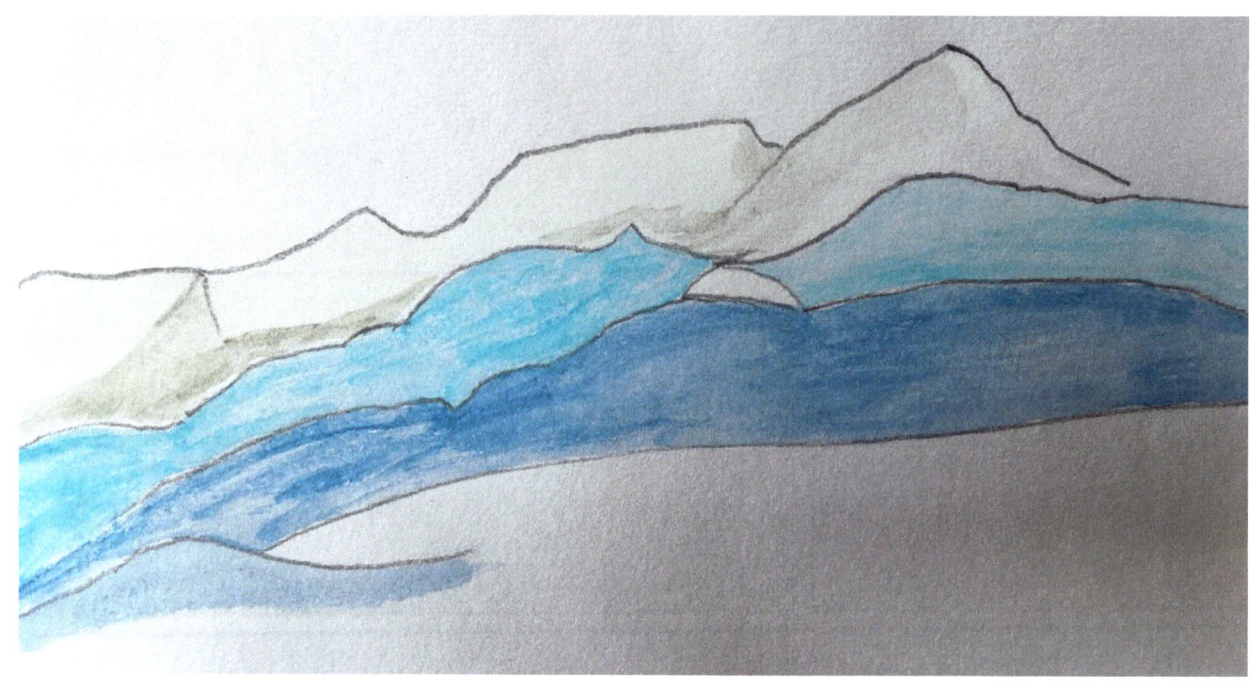

Highlands Mountains © 2019 by Craig Michael Maki

"I have viewed this range of spectacular snowcapped peaks all of my life as they rise thousands of feet above the Summit Valley where Butte, Montana is located."

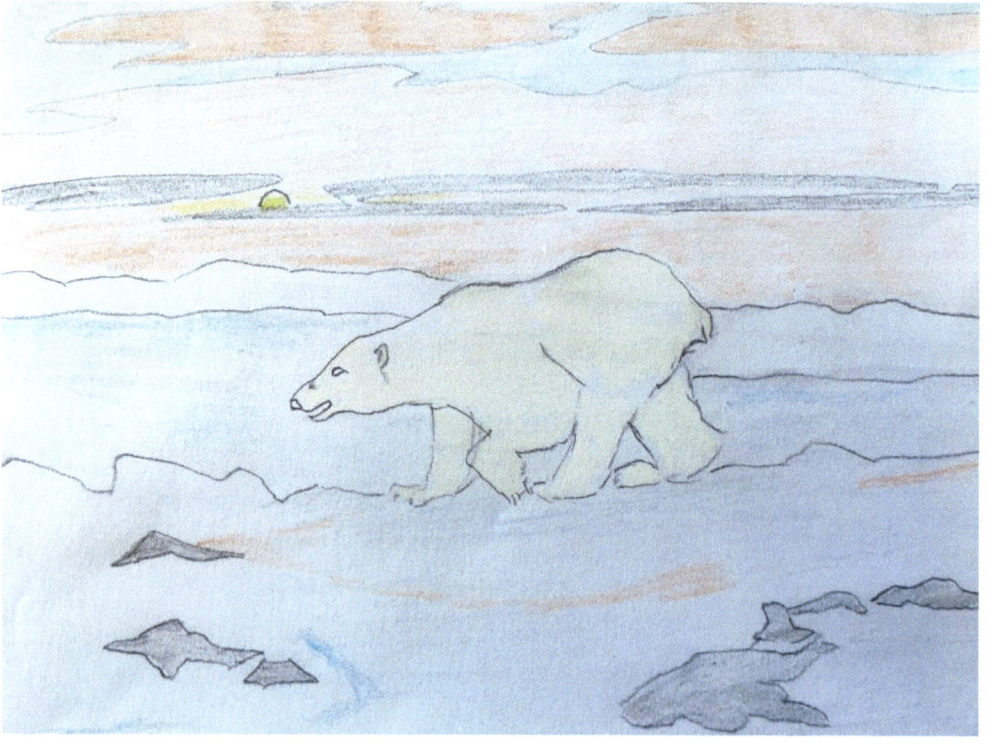

"The largest bear in North America, Polar Bears are a magnificent species that survives where few animals do."

Polar Bear

© 2019 by Craig Michael Maki

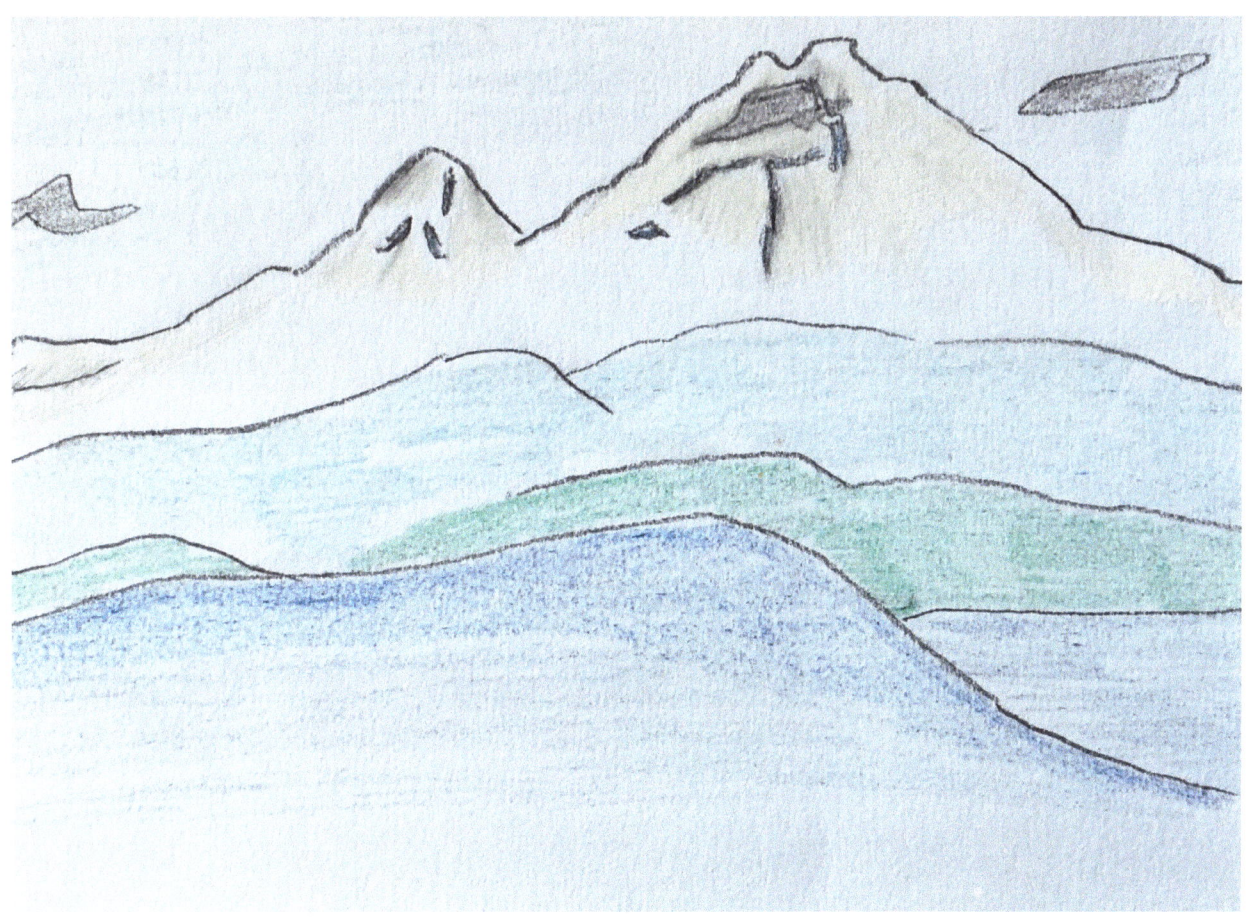

Layered Mountains © 2019 by Craig Michael Maki

"Have you ever noticed successive layers of mountains on the distant horizon? They provide an amazing sense of mystique beckoning further inspection."

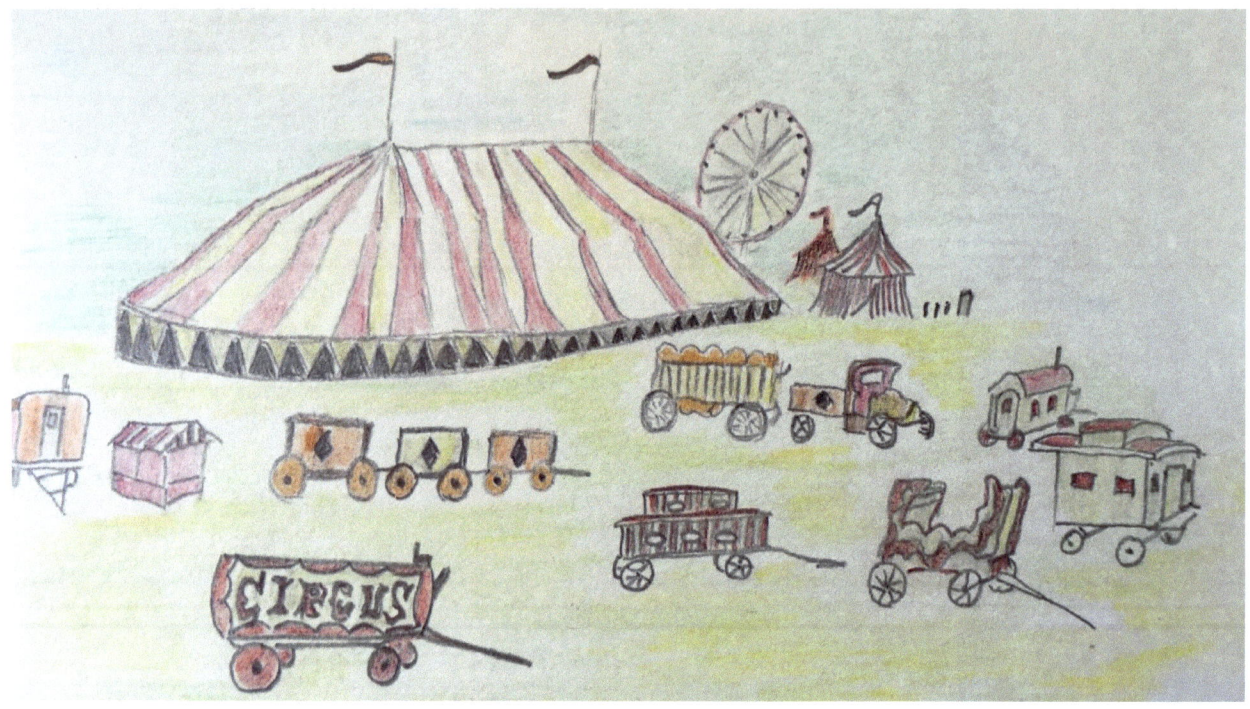

Old Fashioned Circus © 2019 by Craig Michael Maki

"As a child there was nothing like the thrill of the circus when it visited our town. The dazzling spectacle delivered awe and filled our imaginations with worlds beyond our own."

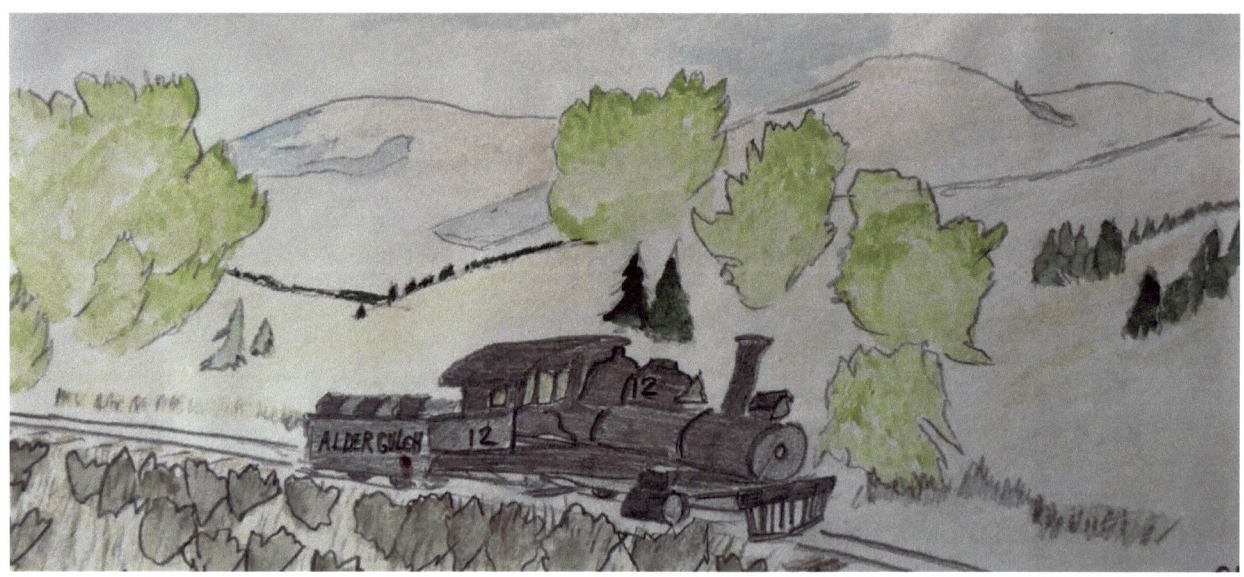

Alder Gulch Train © 2019 by Craig Michael Maki

"I remember the childhood joy I experienced riding behind the old steam-driven locomotive pulling the passenger cars of the Alder Gulch Train between Virginia City and Nevada City."

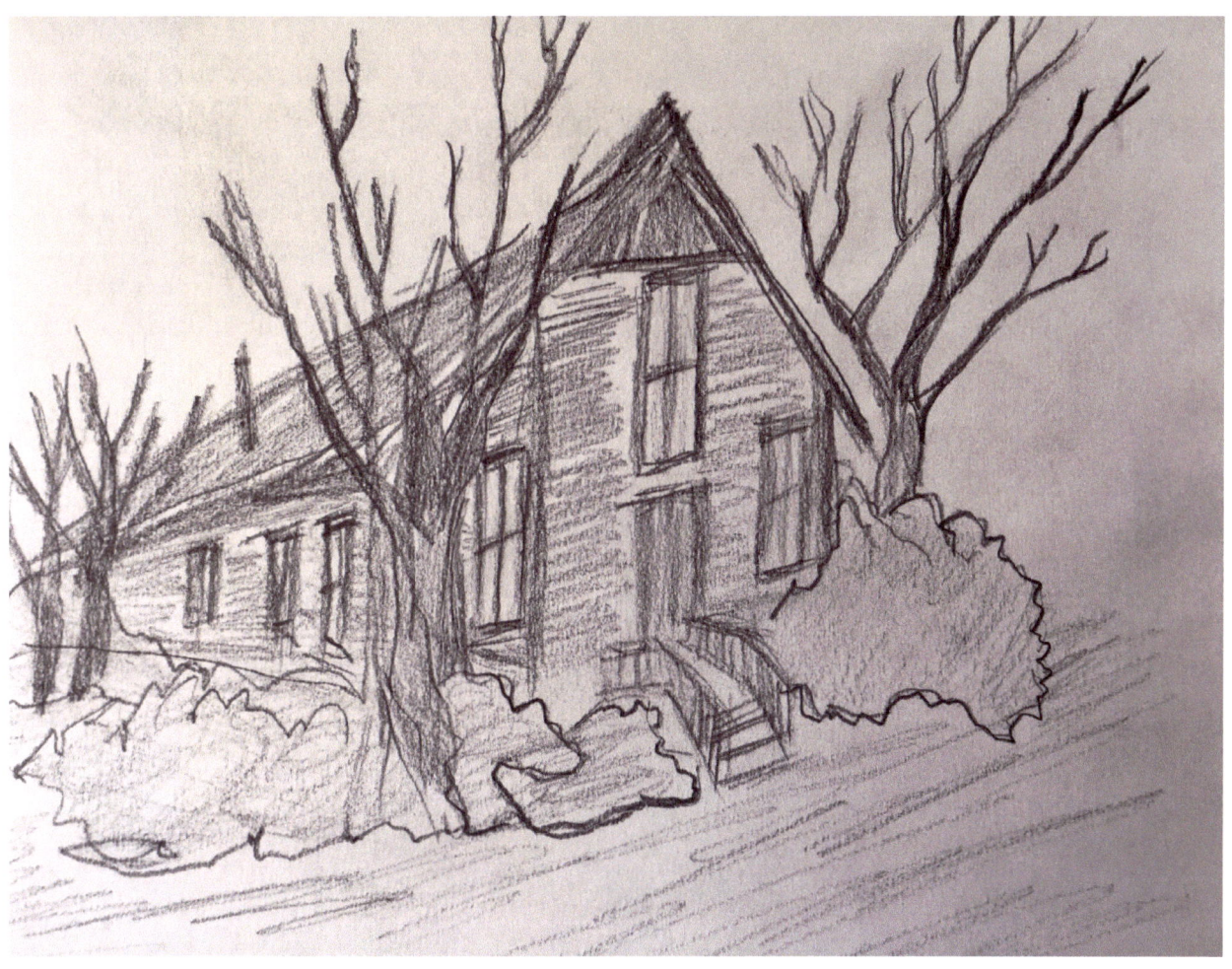

One Room School House © 2019 by Craig Michael Maki

"I remember memories of my father telling us about the many schools he attended growing up – including one room school houses where all grades were taught at the same time by one teacher."

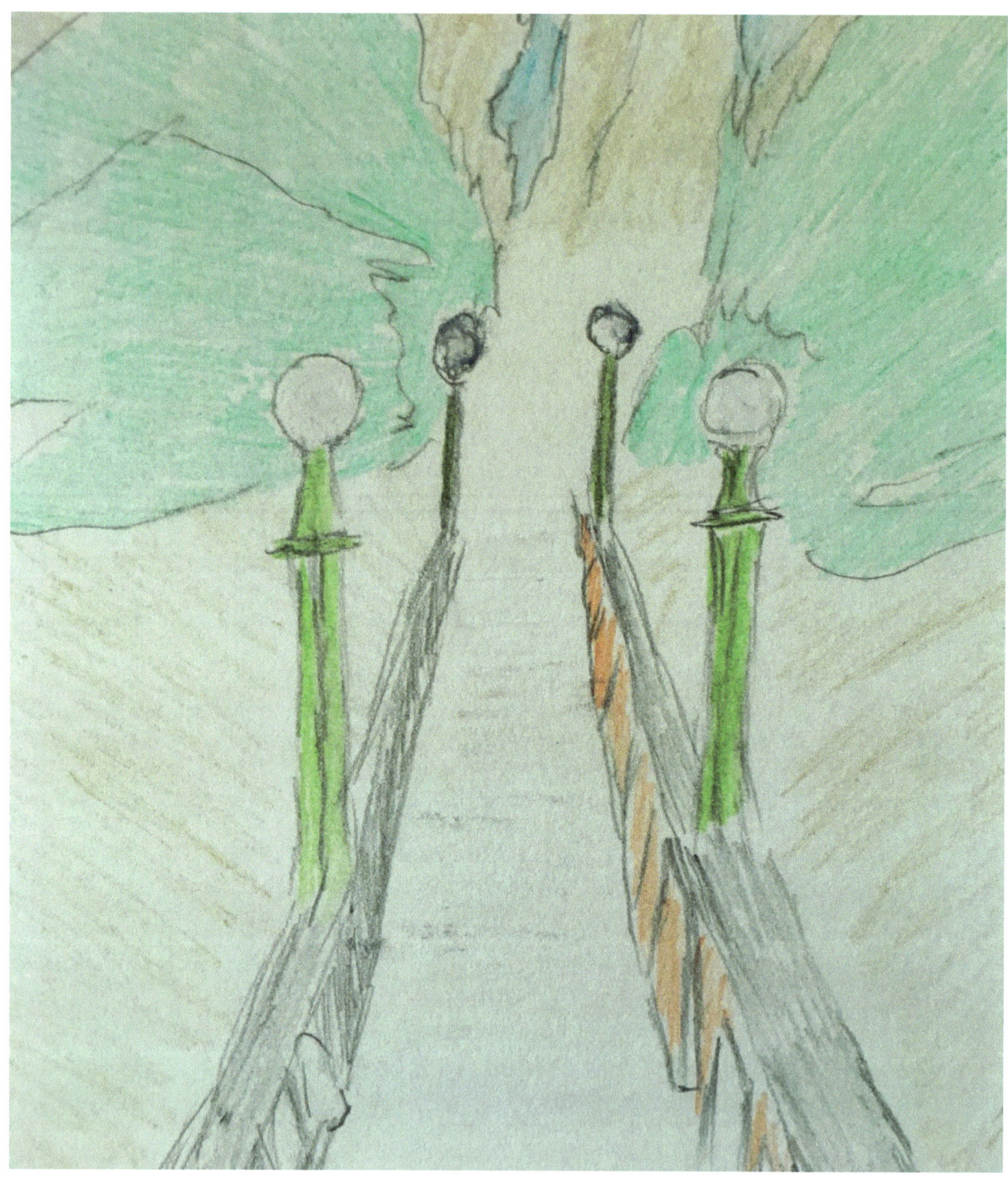

Bridge to the Arboretum © 2019 by Craig Michael Maki

"Crossing this quaint bridge to the arboretum at the University of Washington in Seattle is a wonderful experience at early dawn."

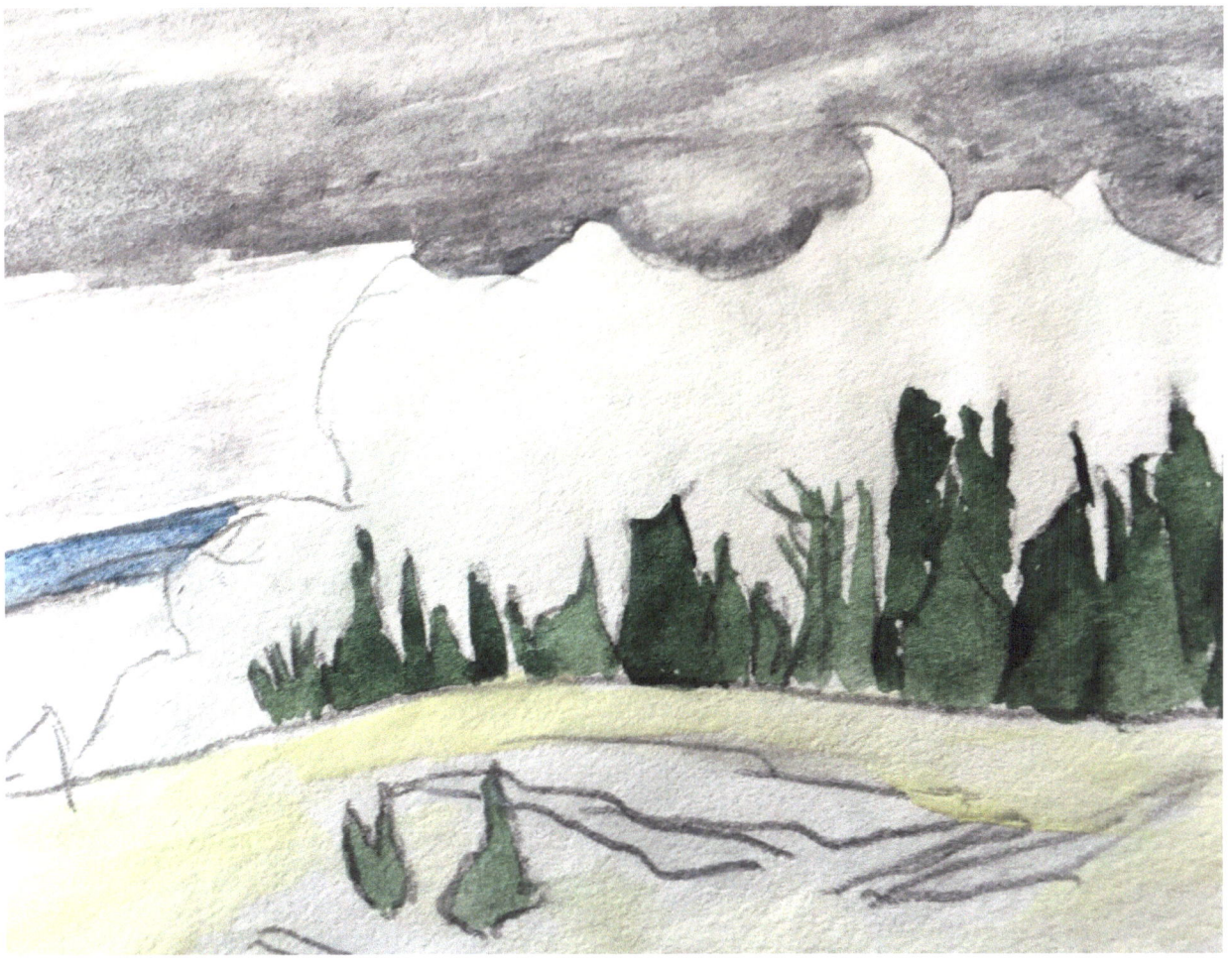

Big Sky Meadow © 2019 by Craig Michael Maki

"Montana is known as the Big Sky Country for good reason. Some days it seems like the sky is so vast that it is ready to swallow up the mountains, the forests, and the meadows."

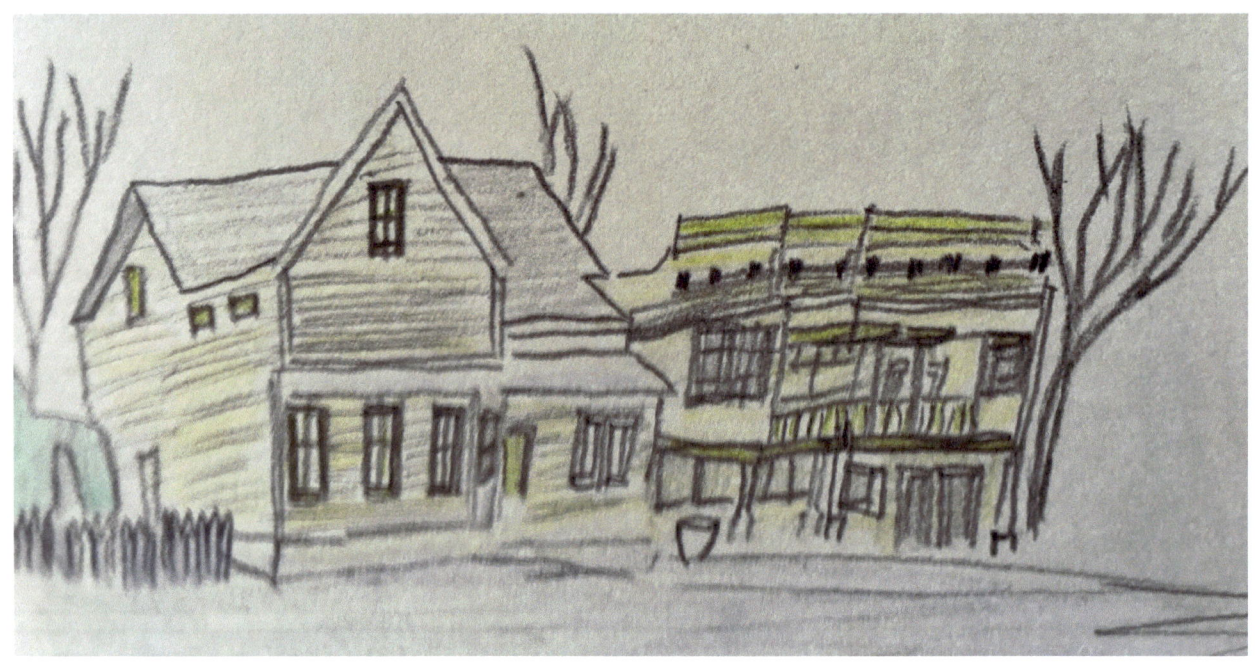

Rustic Hideaway © 2019 by Craig Michael Maki

"Buildings of a bygone era call us to remember times that weren't so complicated – at least that is the myth we like to hold in our minds when pondering the quaint history of old dilapidated buildings."

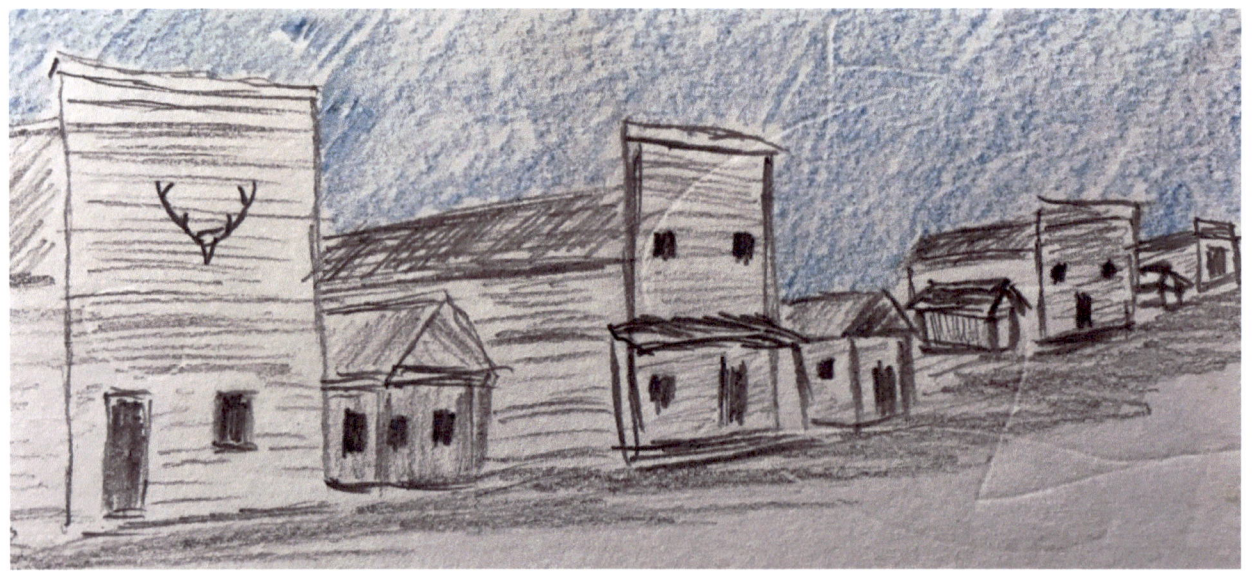

Ghostly Main Street © 2019 by Craig Michael Maki

"The old ghost towns of the West invoke feelings of intrigue as we ponder the lives that were once so invested in building towns that now stand empty of the promises they once held."

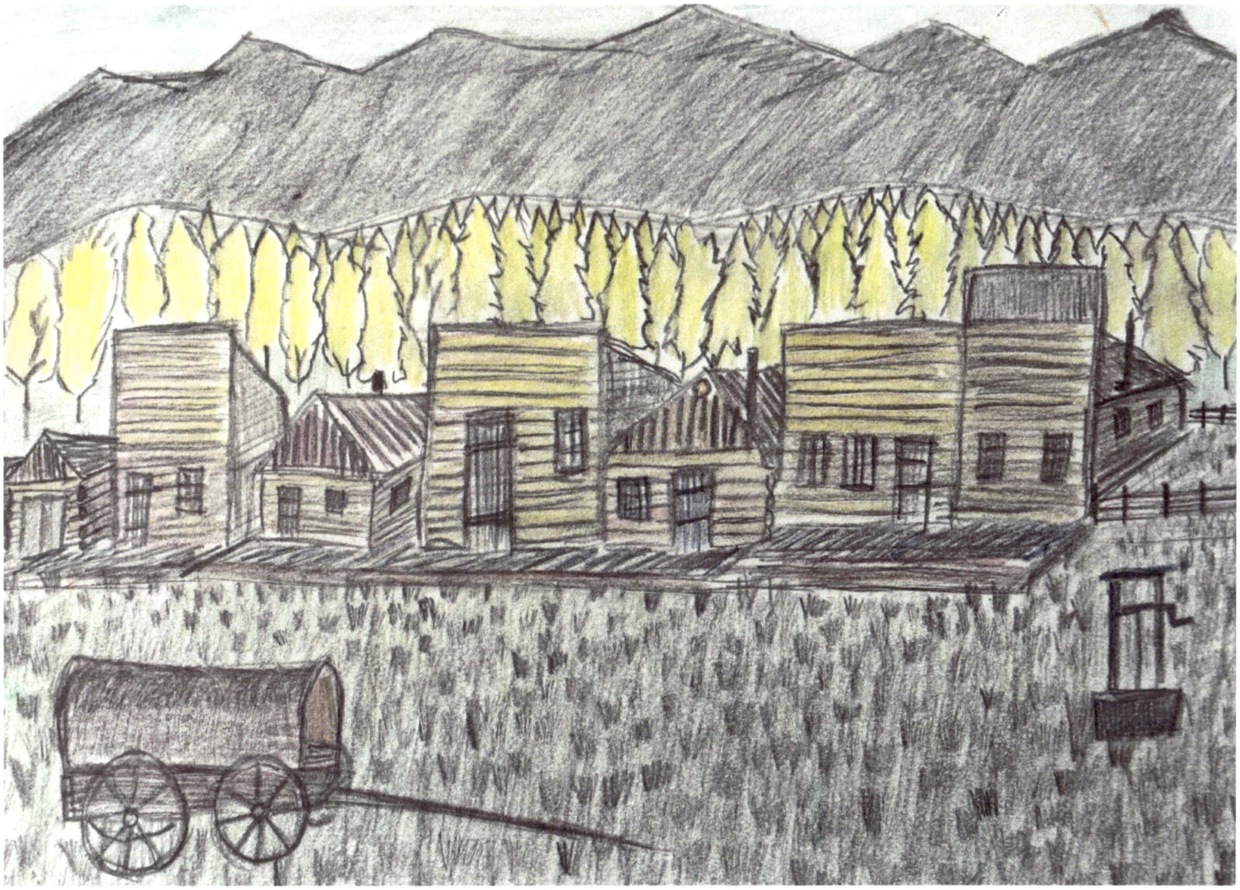

Old West Gold Town © 2019 by Craig Michael Maki

"Boom and bust silver and gold strikes built a majority of the old towns of the American West. Today ghost towns remind us of the more prosperous times once found in these rough and tumble mining camps."

"The boarding house was the residence of many a miner and lumbermen – offering room and board at an affordable price."

Old Boarding House
© 2019 by Craig Michael Maki

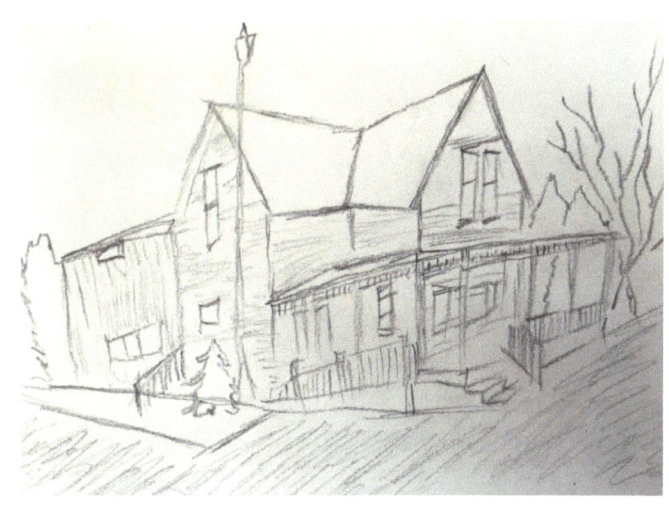

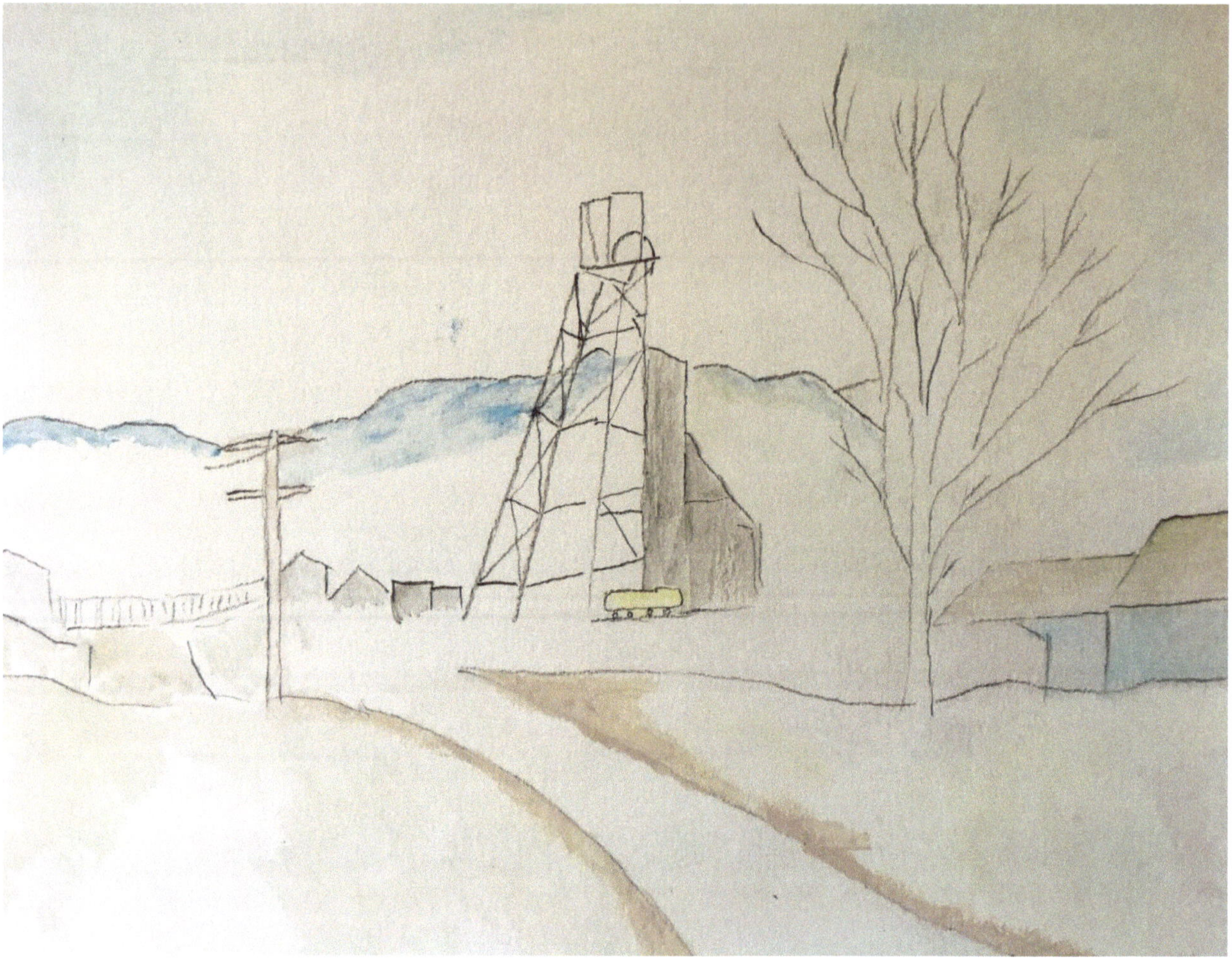

Butte Icon　　　　　　　　　　　　　　　　　　　　© 2019 by Craig Michael Maki

"Mining gallows frames pepper the city of Butte, Montana –known as the 'Richest Hill on Earth'."

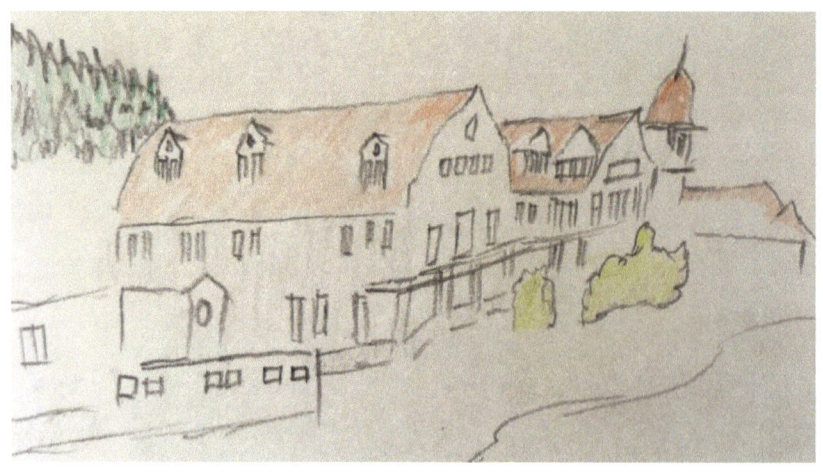

"This historical hot spring and hotel date back to the late 1800's."

Boulder Hot Springs Hotel
© 2019 by Craig Michael Maki

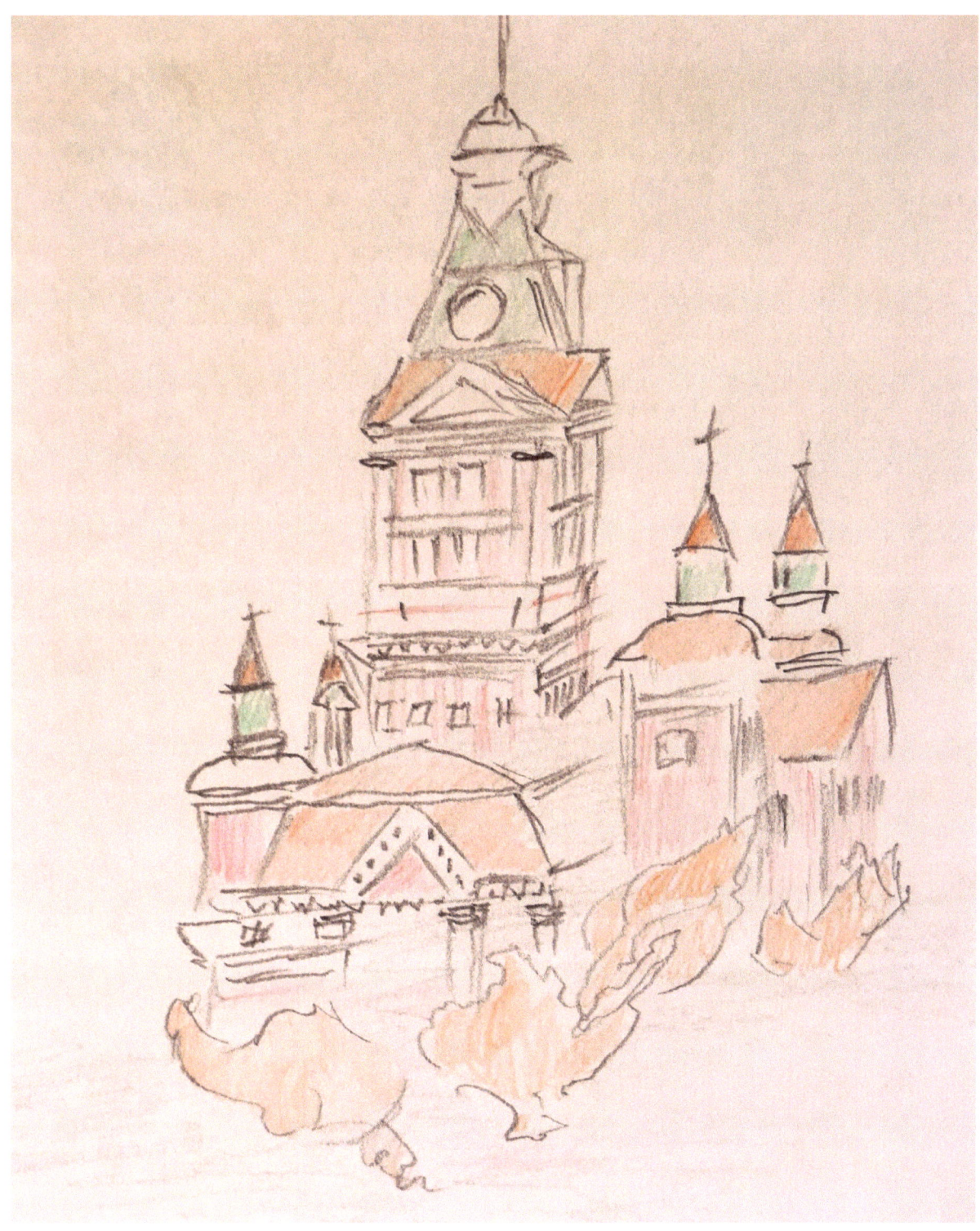

Old City Hall © 2019 by Craig Michael Maki

"Travel to Bellingham, WA and you can still see the towering old city hall in all of its Victorian glory."

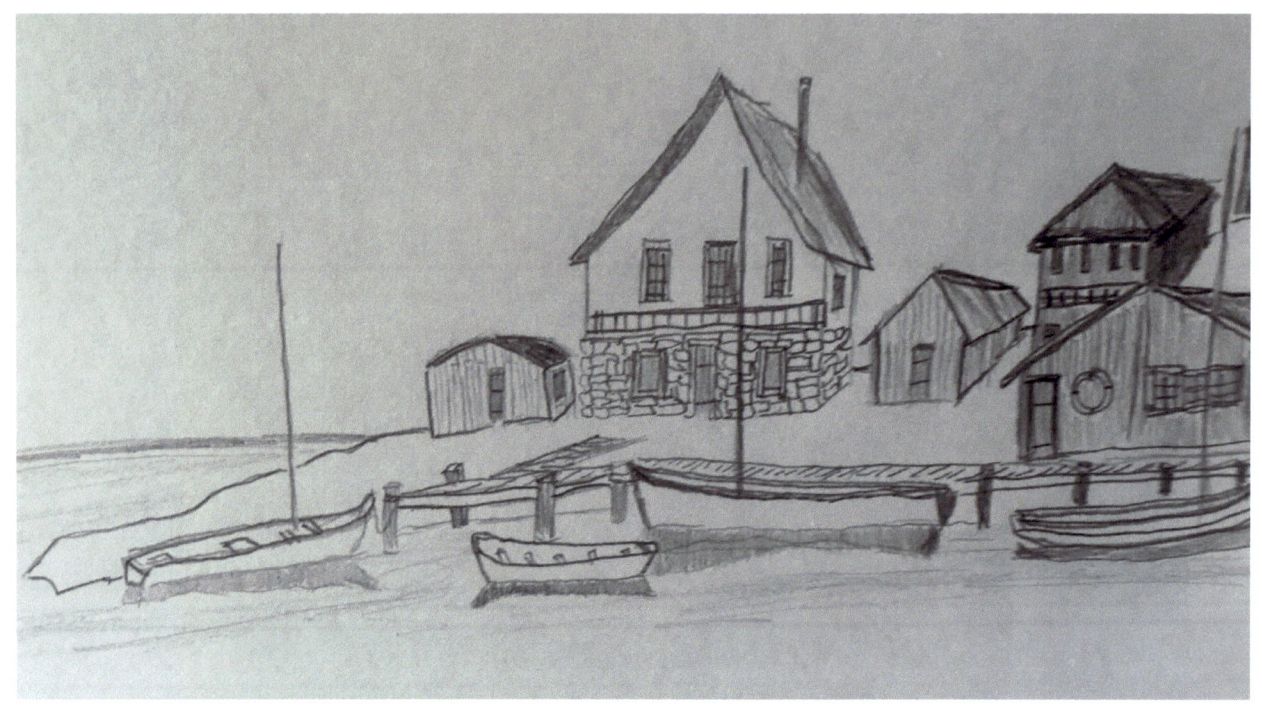

Northern Fishing Village © 2019 by Craig Michael Maki

"I love quaint remote fishing villages built with the labor by those who make their living from the sea."

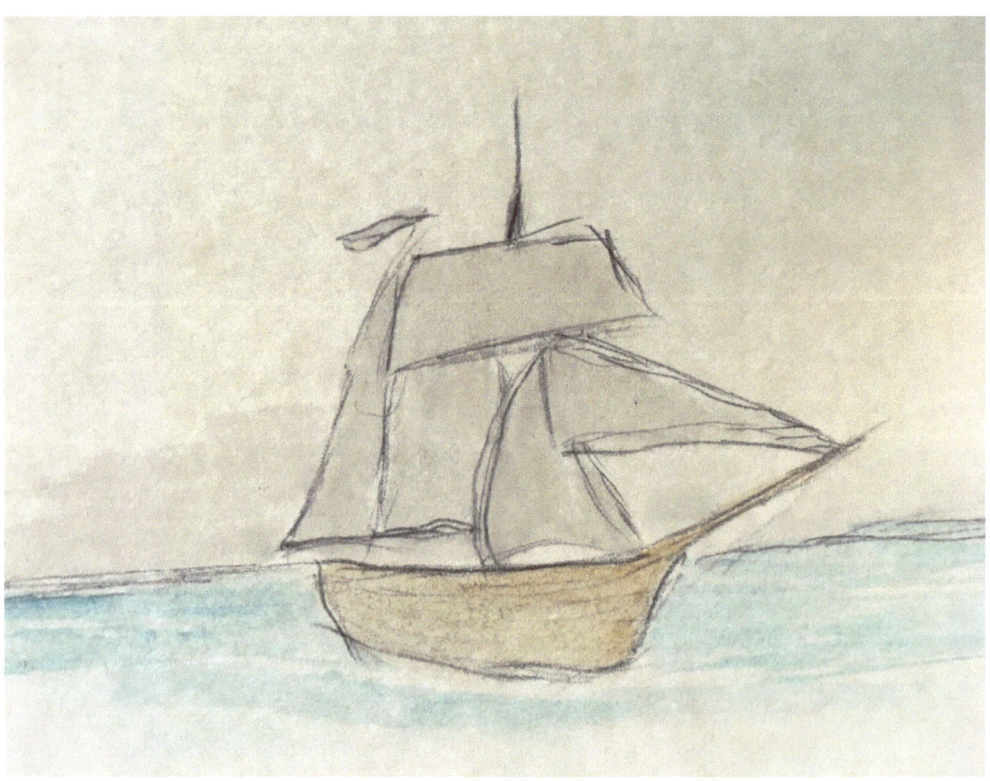

"When you think about it, the positioning of the numerous sails of a ship is an engineering marvel."

Full Sail
© 2019 by Craig Michael Maki

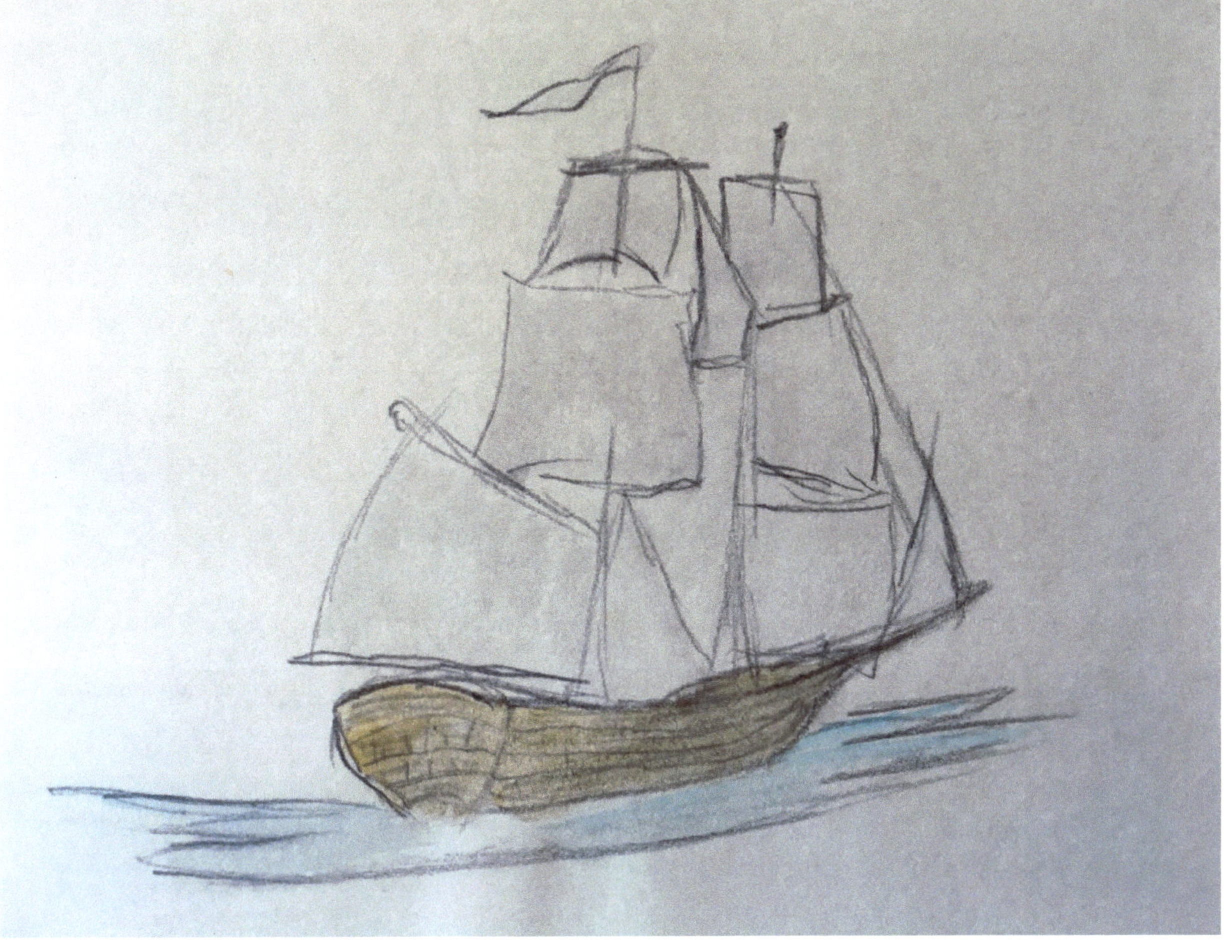

Homebound Voyage   © 2019 by Craig Michael Maki

"The old tall sailing ships were perhaps one of the most unique forms of traveling back home."

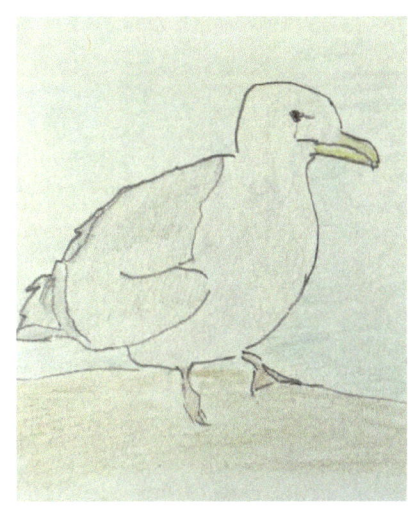

"This amazing seabird can be found along shores, following ships at sea, and for sure where ever there is a concentration of a food source."

Seagull
© 2019 by Craig Michael Maki

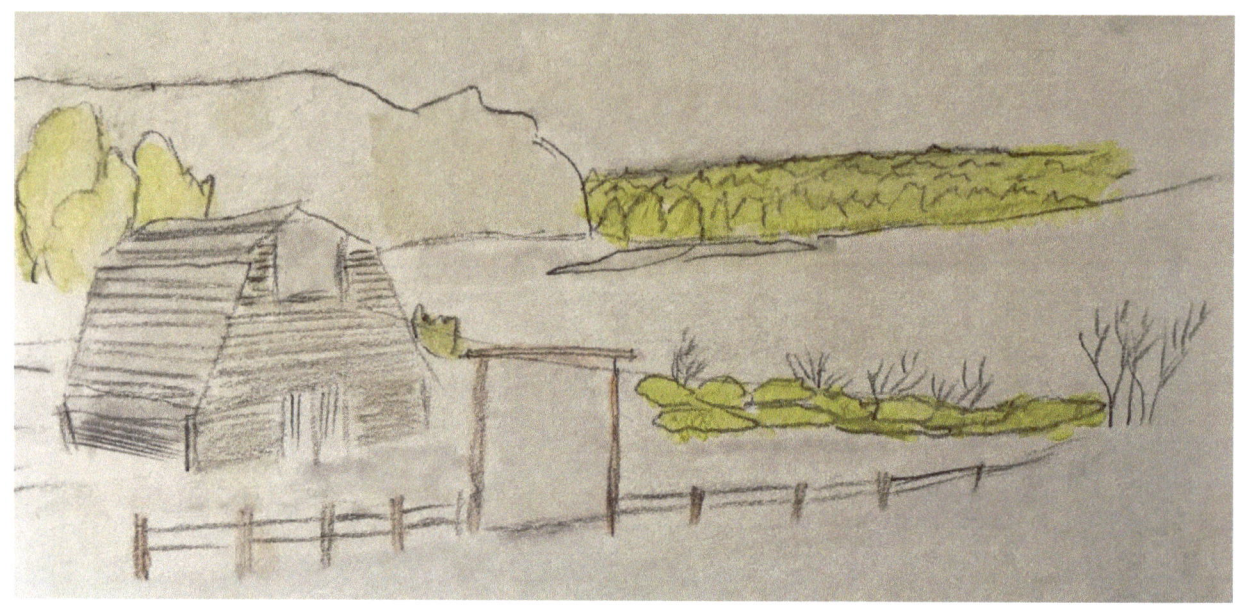

Rustic Barn © 2019 by Craig Michael Maki

"Old rustic ranches are an eye catching artist's' dream – especially they are nestled in a high mountain valley rimmed with peaks and forests."

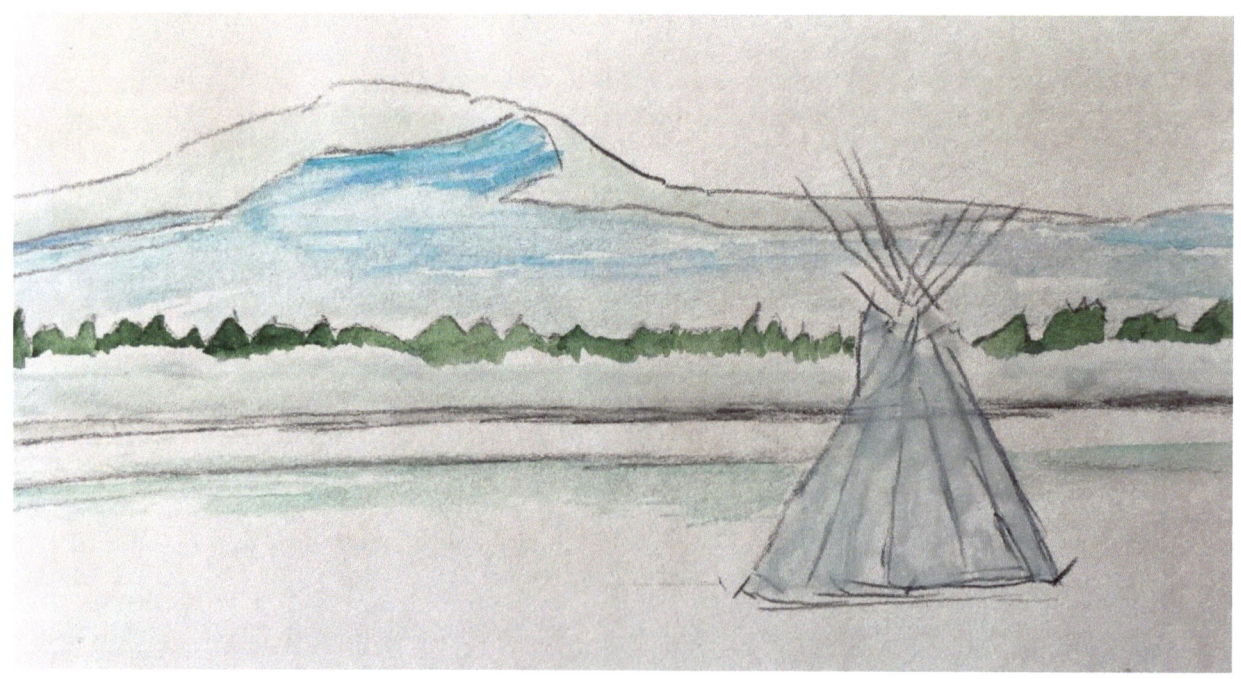

Lone Teepee © 2019 by Craig Michael Maki

"You can almost hear the elk bugling in the forest beyond this teepee in a high mountain valley."

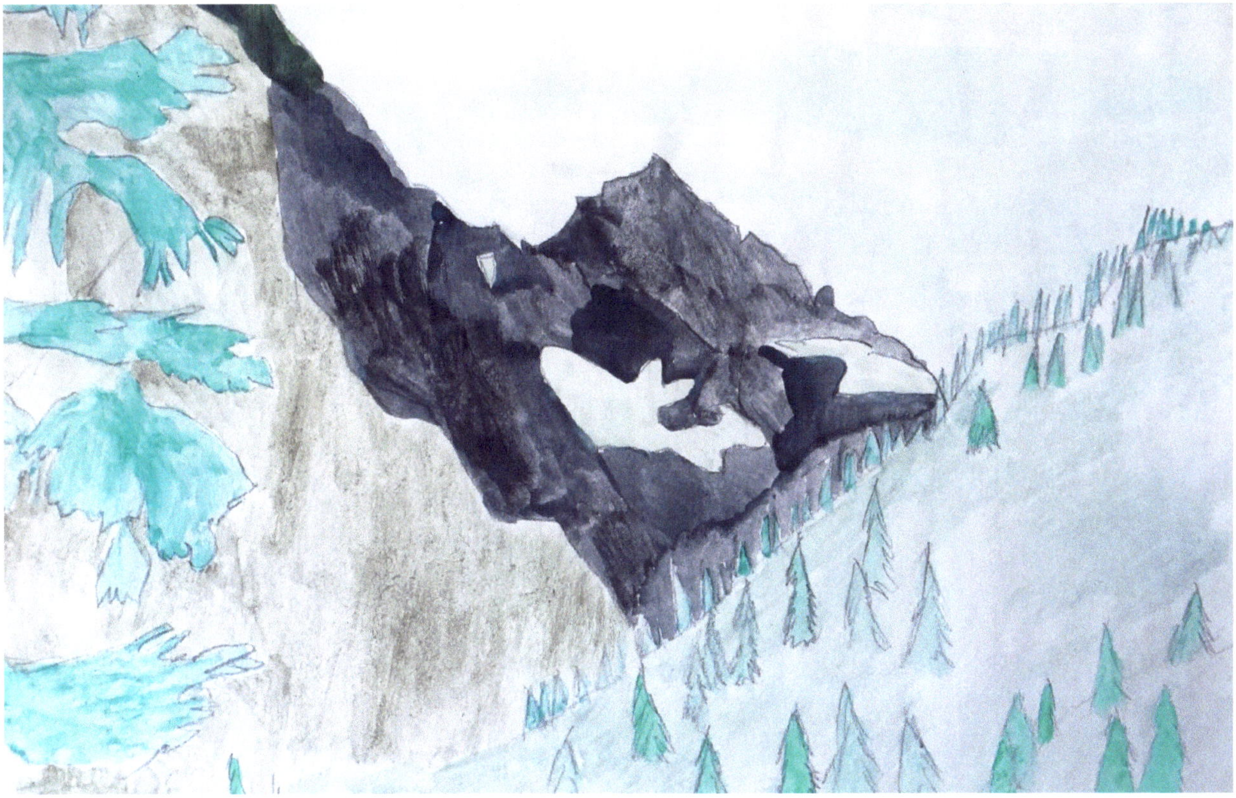

Glacial Peak © 2019 by Craig Michael Maki

"Glaciers are nature's timeless carving tools – cutting sharp edges into the ancient mountain rock."

"The sound of a babbling brook calms the soul and reminds us that sometimes it is the simple things that matter."

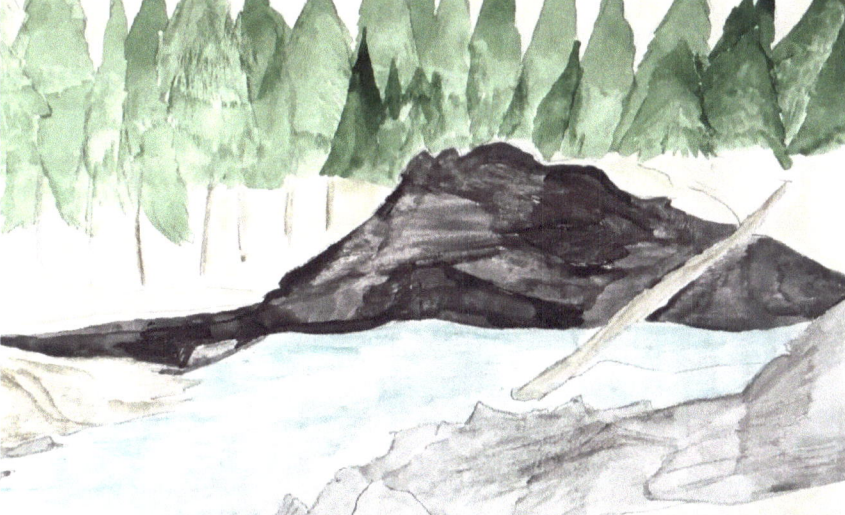

Wild Creek

© 2019 by Craig Michael Maki

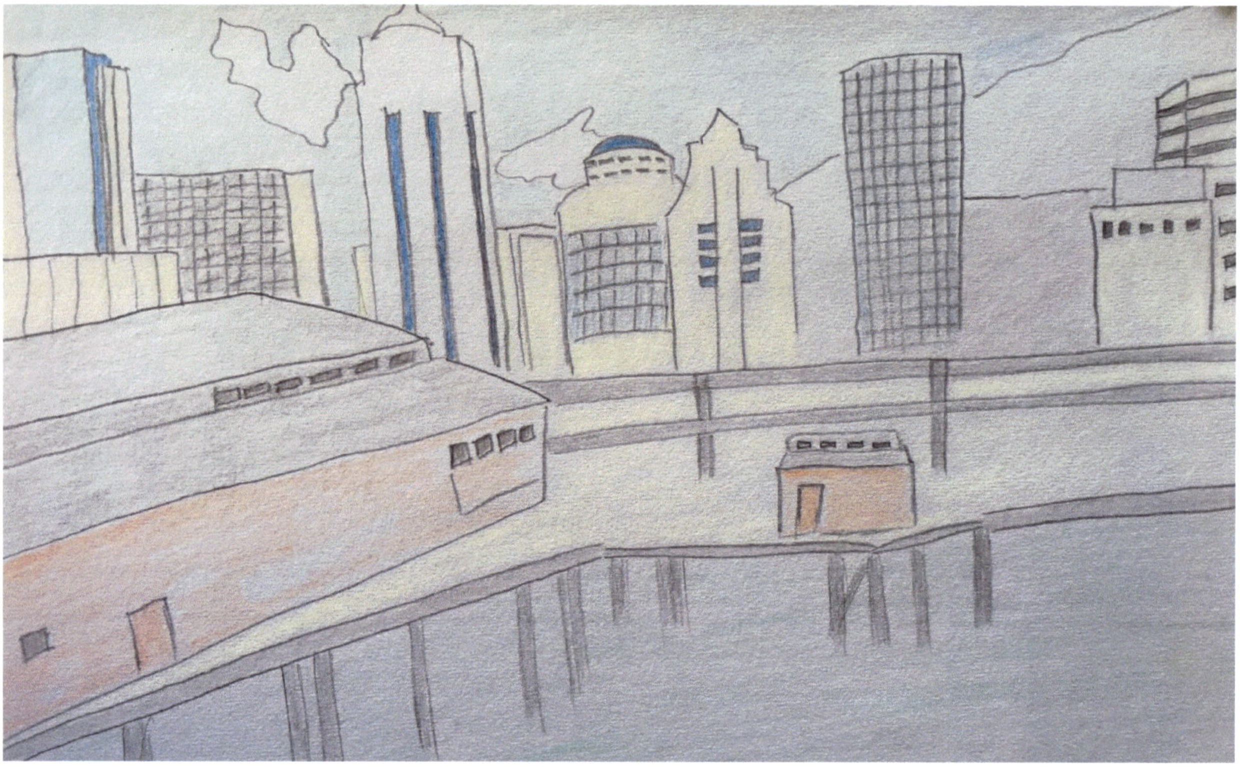

Seattle Waterfront © 2019 by Craig Michael Maki

"Seattle definitely is the Emerald City – and its impressive location on the edge of Puget Sound blends the best of both worlds of land and sea."

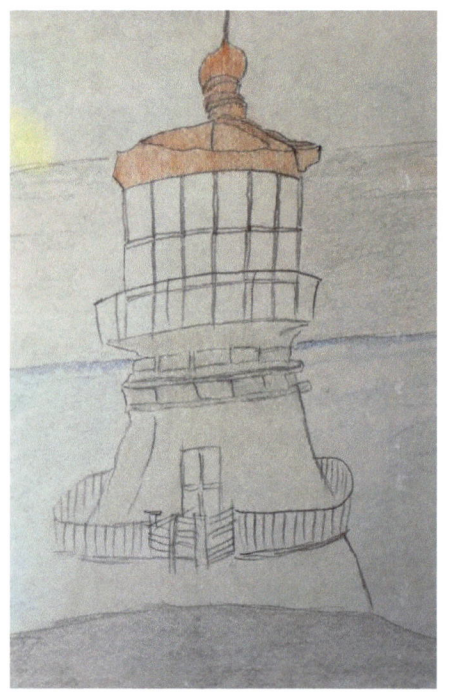

"Head north across the Golden Gate Bridge and hang a left, and drive West for an hour, and you'll arrive at a magnificent lighthouse overlooking the Pacific Ocean."

Point Reyes Lighthouse
© 2019 by Craig Michael Maki

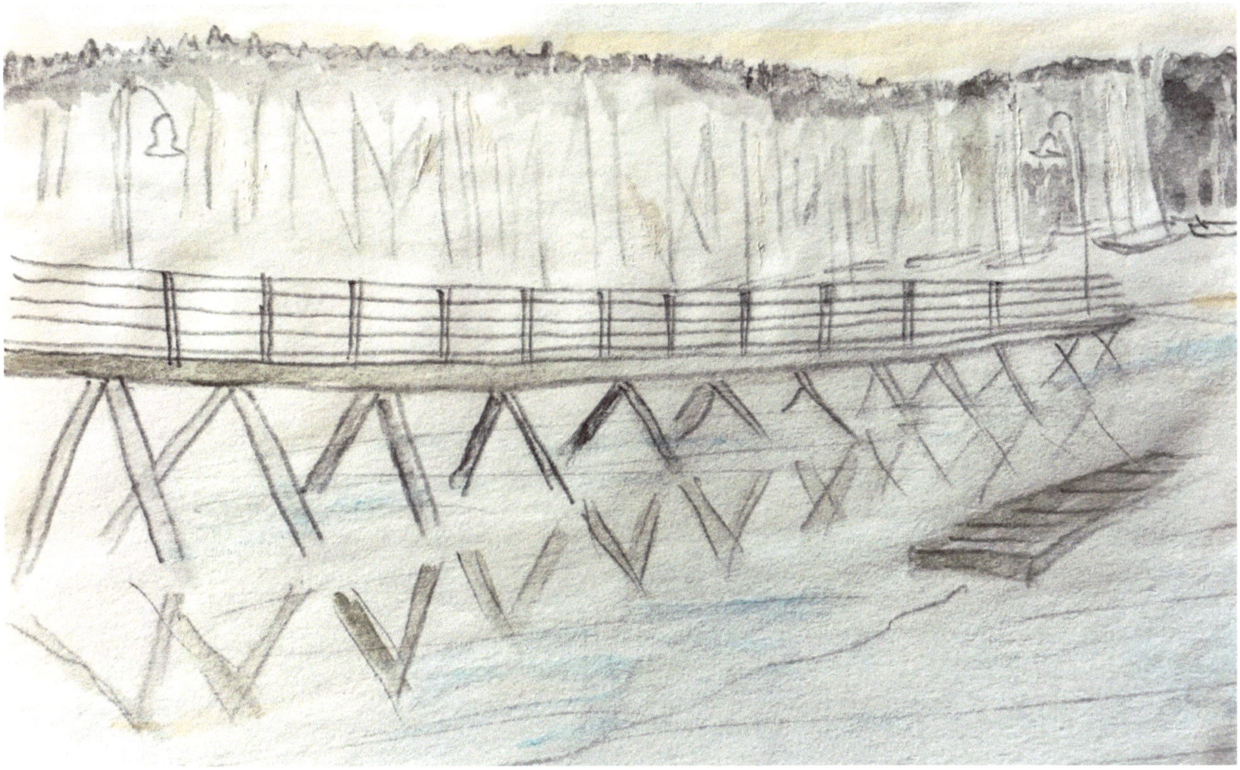

Dockside   © 2019 by Craig Michael Maki

"Docks are an amazing interface between the land and the sea – a unique jumping off point for sailors, a platform to fish, and a perfect spot to get away from it all."

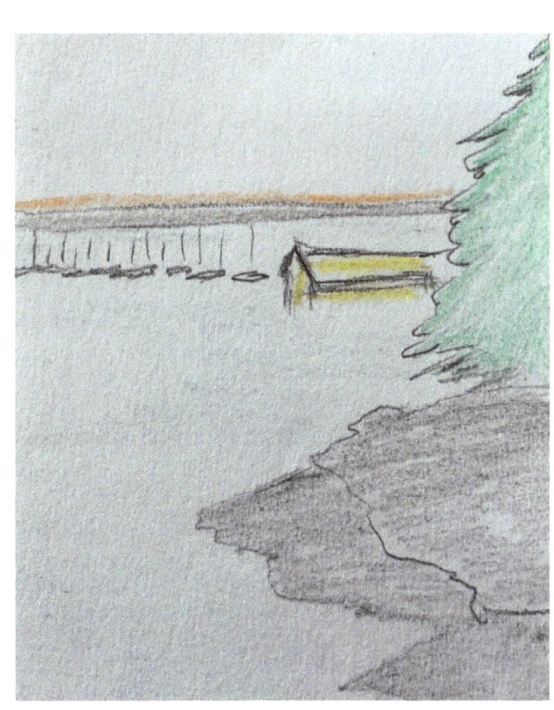

"I remember the day I was walking up the shoreline, came around a point containing a beautiful old tree, and there was a picturesque marina stock-full of sailboats."

Shoreline Marina
© 2019 by Craig Michael Maki

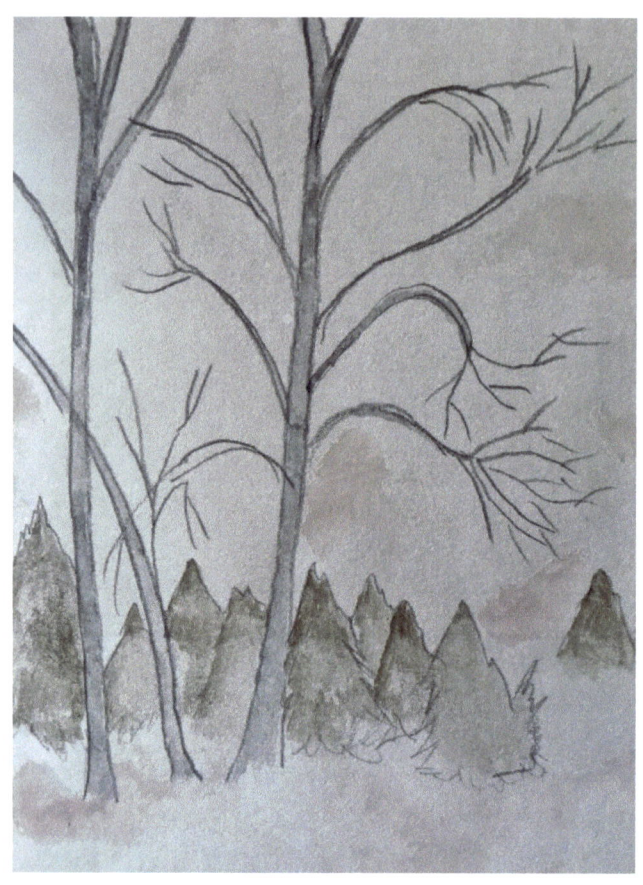

"Long after the leaves have fallen from the trees, and the cold wind whistles through the branches, nature reminds us that rest is crucial to the growth of life."

Winter Aspen
© 2019 by Craig Michael Maki

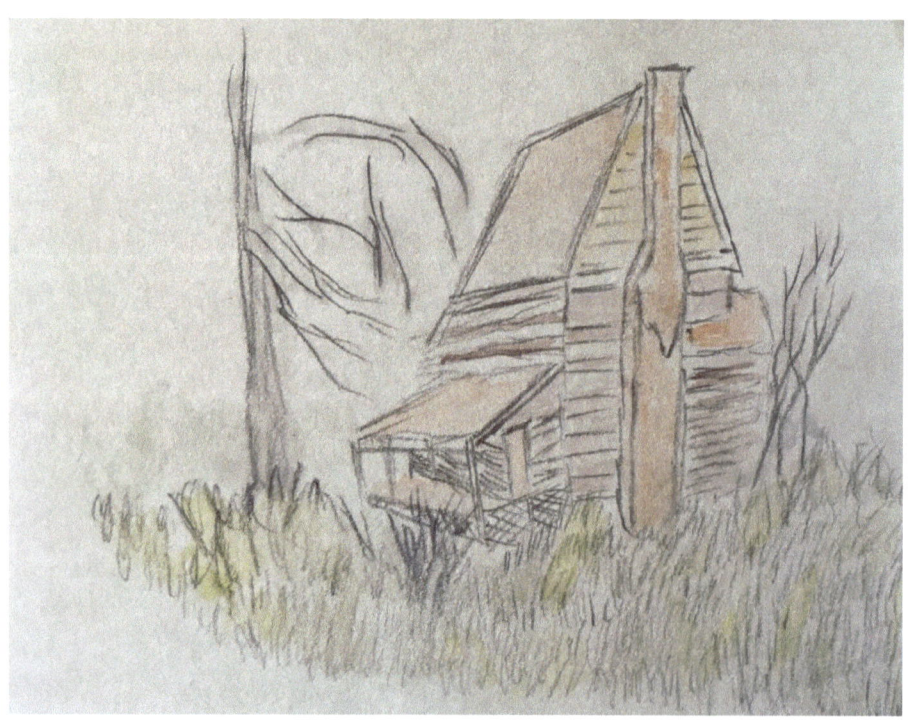

"Weathered old cabins tell their own story of days gone by – but still keeping many secrets."

Settler's Cabin
© 2019 by Craig Michael Maki

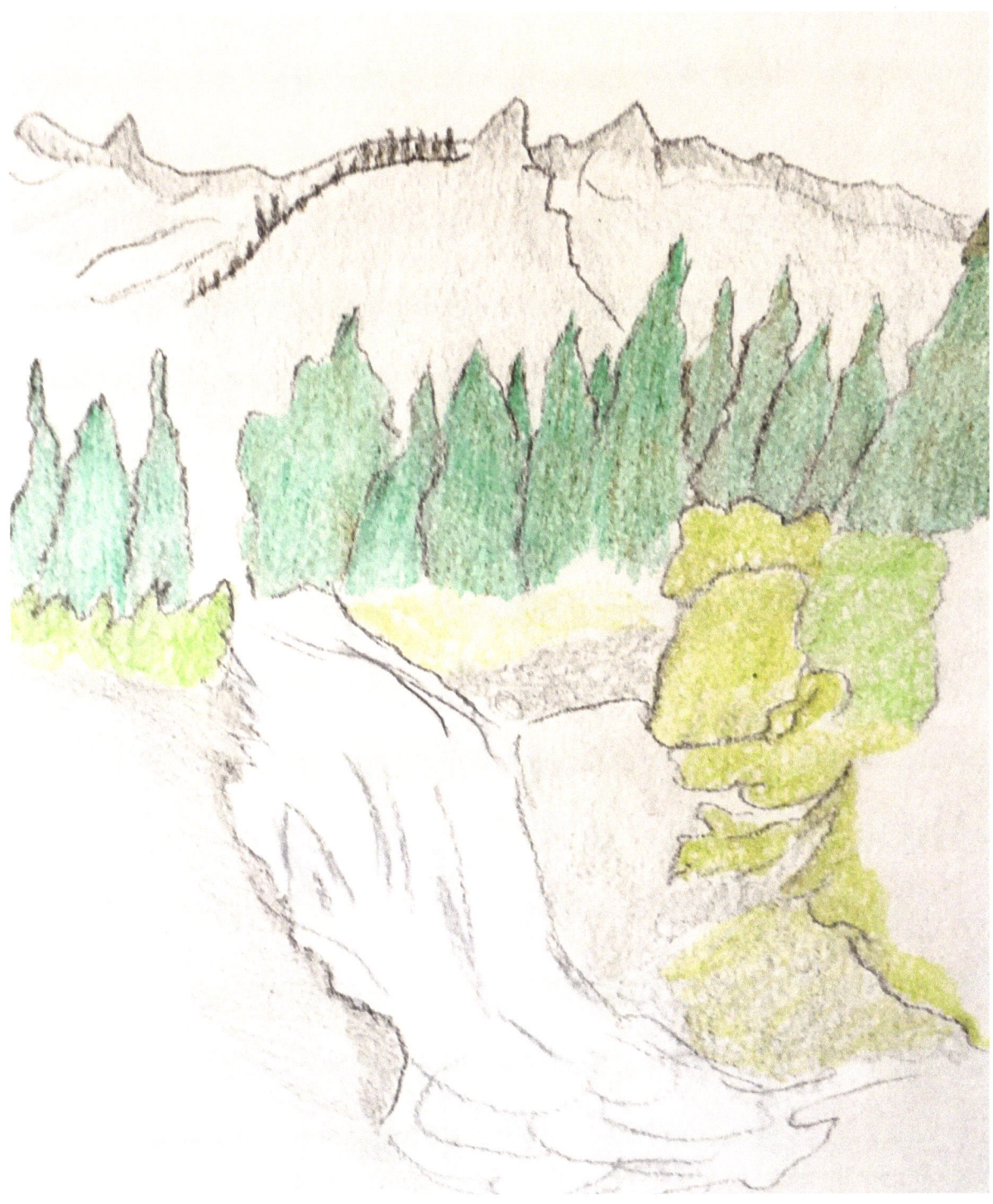

Pristine Falls © 2019 by Craig Michael Maki

"The refreshing splendor of wilderness waterfalls is unparalleled. It is no wonder that hikers have been seeking out their soothing roar and wondrous visual spectacles for centuries."

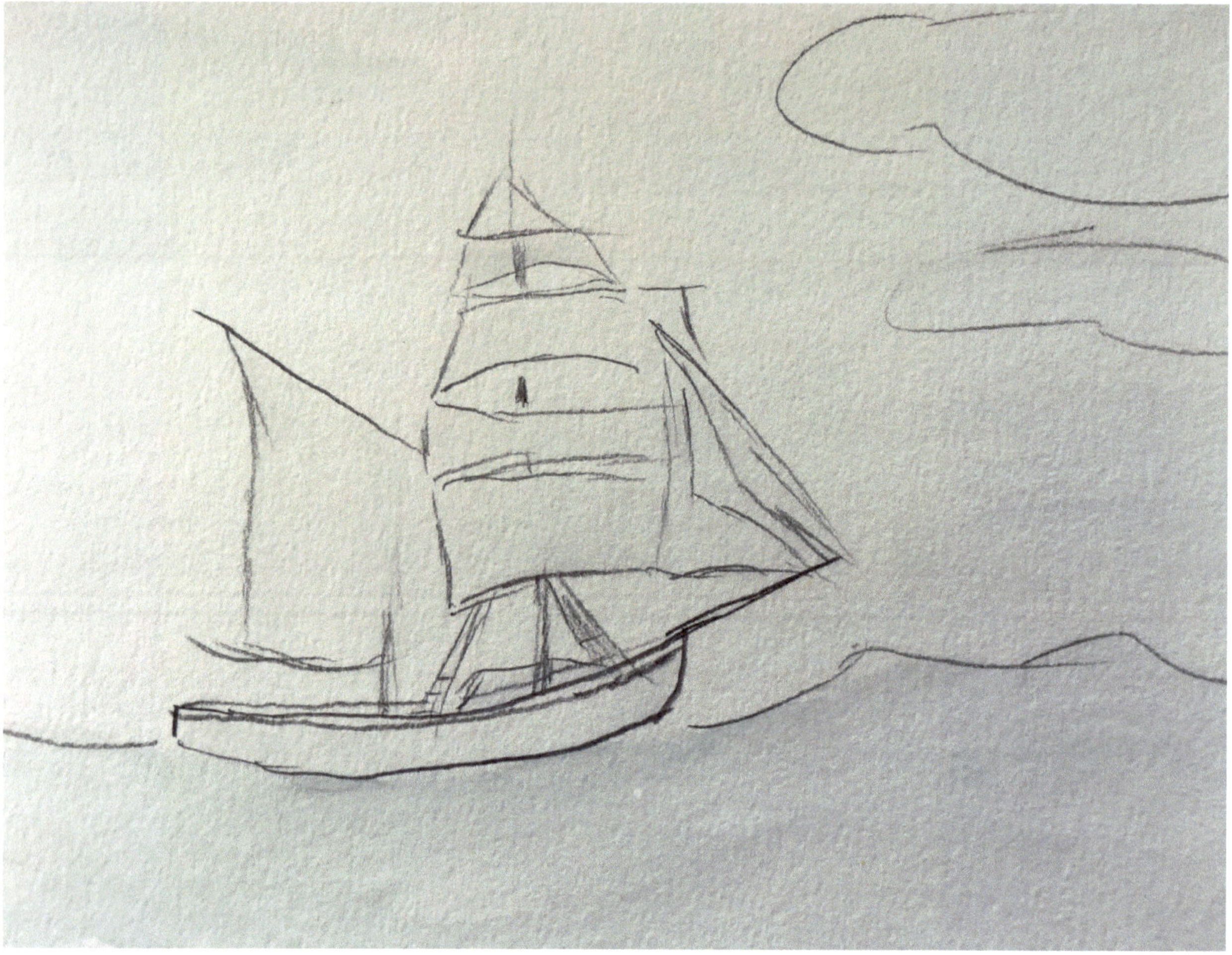

Stormy Skies Ahead © 2019 by Craig Michael Maki

"The wind powers these magnificent sailing ships, and yet the winds bring in storms that can devastate and wreak havoc with these sea vessels."

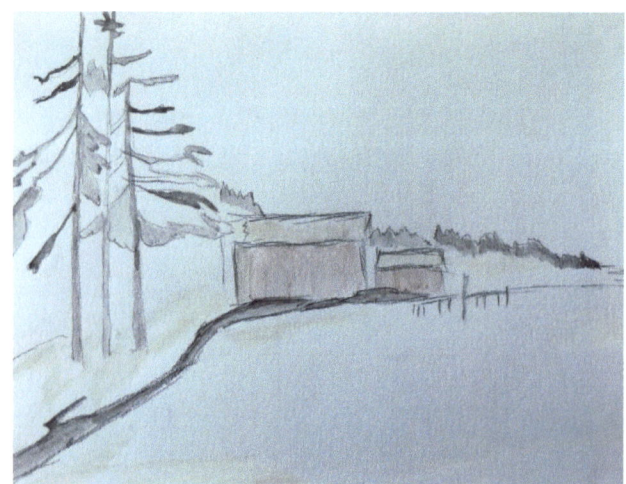

"LaConner, Washington is a perfect example of an old fishing village that has been well preserved while maintaining its economic base."

LaConner Boathouse
© 2019 by Craig Michael Maki

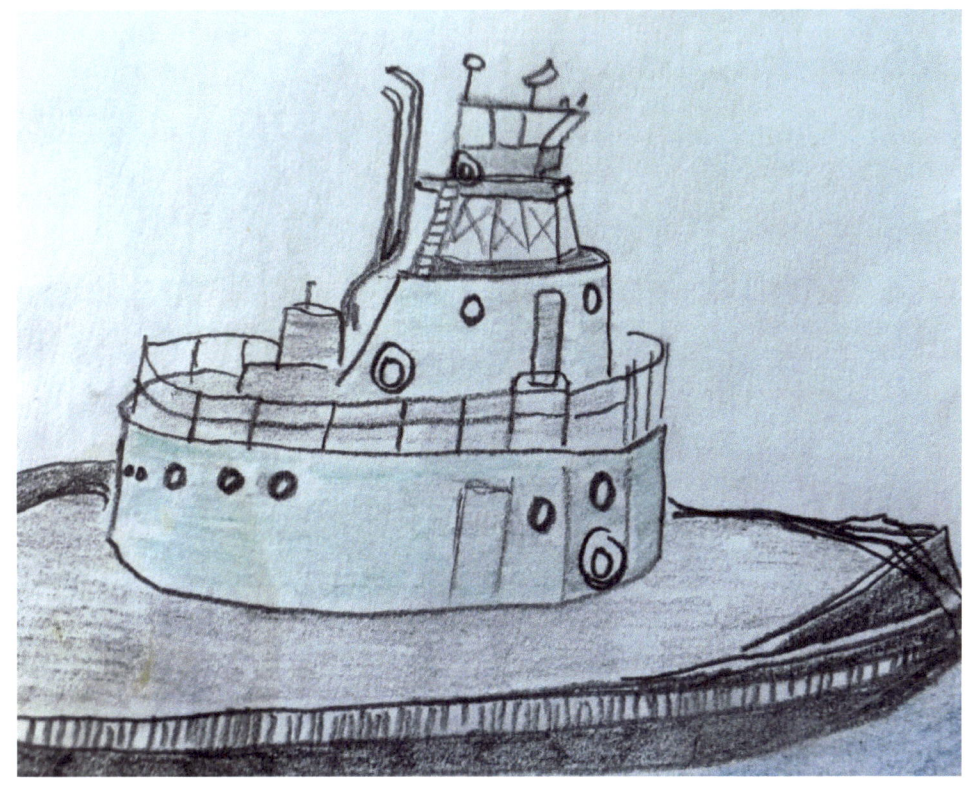

"Recently I visited the Hiram Chittenden Locks in Seattle. I was thrilled to see this old Tugboat towing a huge barge full of rock."

Tugboat in the Locks
© 2019 by Craig Michael Maki

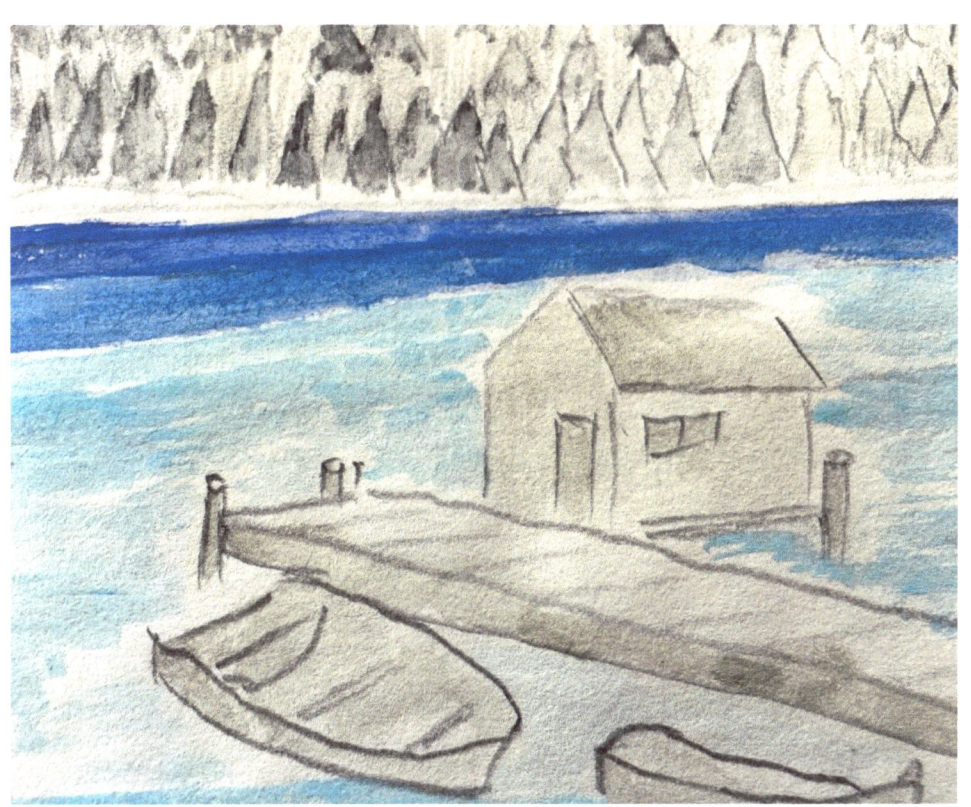

"Finding a convenient place to moor your boat is a challenge that can be rewarded if you employ a little patience and diligence."

Moored
© 2019 by Craig Michael Maki

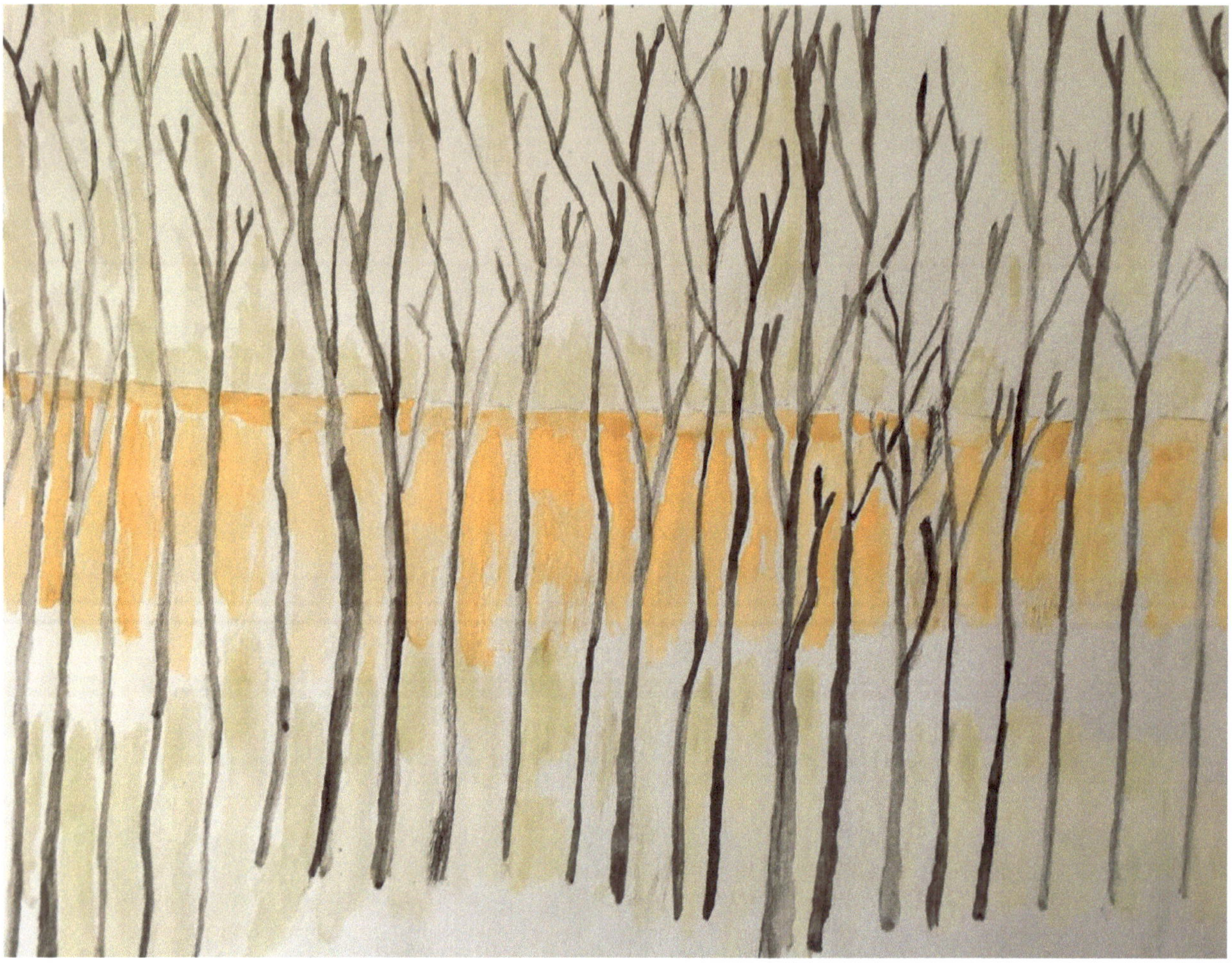

Parallel Forest © 2019 by Craig Michael Maki

"Sometimes the geometry of the forest is what captivates the eye. It's amazing when you think about the ability of trees to grow exactly perpendicular to the ground. When they are somewhat evenly spaced, they create a parallel sight that is something to behold."

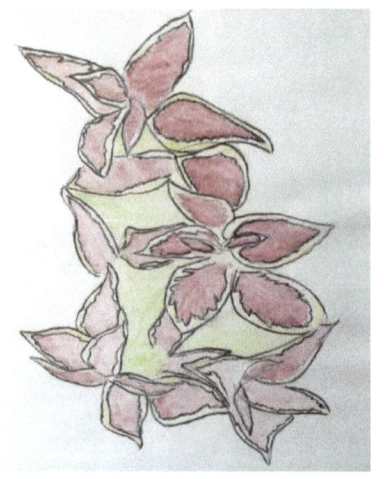

"Sometimes I love to distill something down to its most basic form -- in this case the basic outline of the leaf and the contrasting color contained within it."

Leaves
© 2019 by Craig Michael Maki

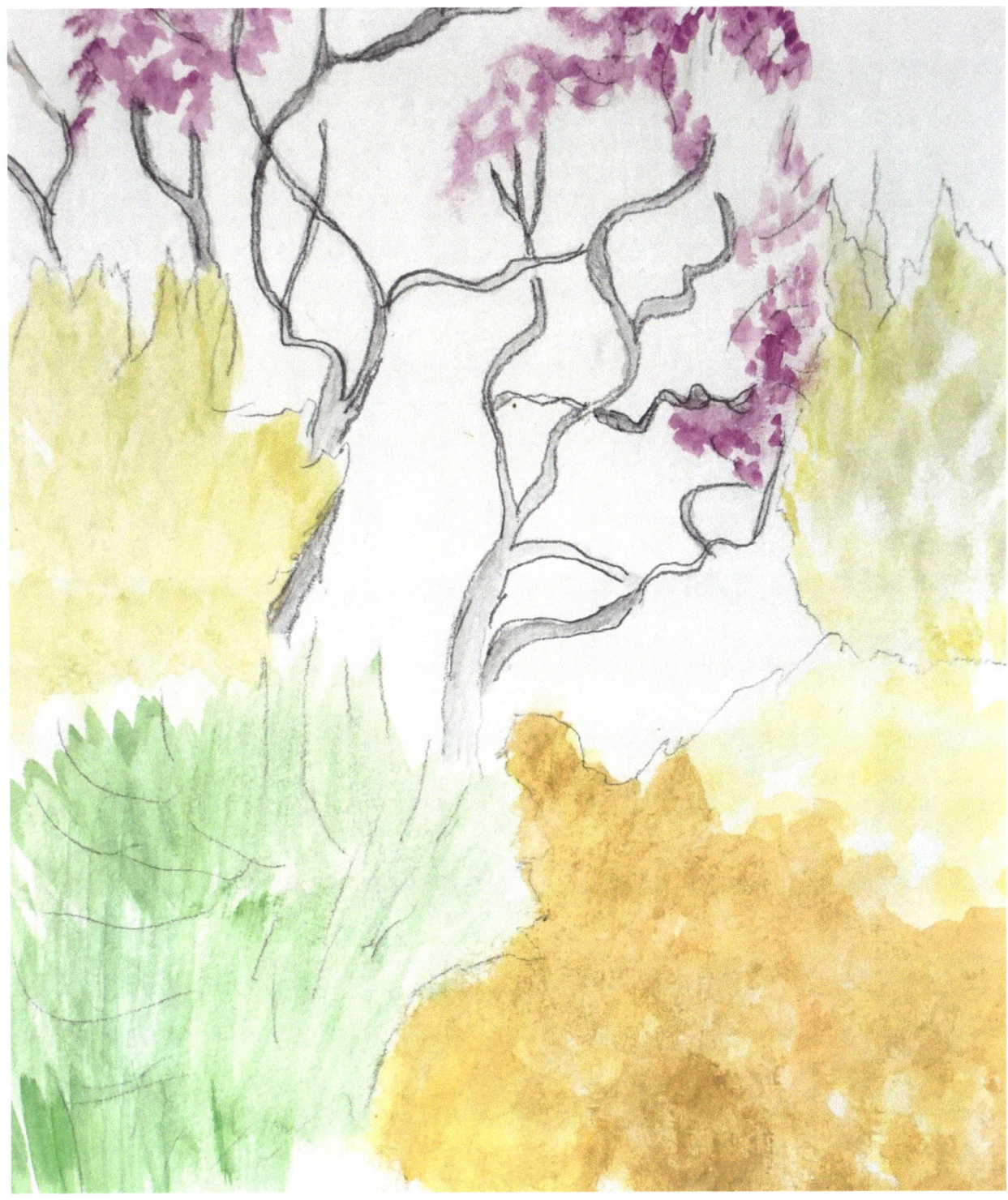

Impressions © 2019 by Craig Michael Maki

"Sometimes I use an impressionist approach to my painting – focusing on the subtle color and general form rather than every detail of a scene."

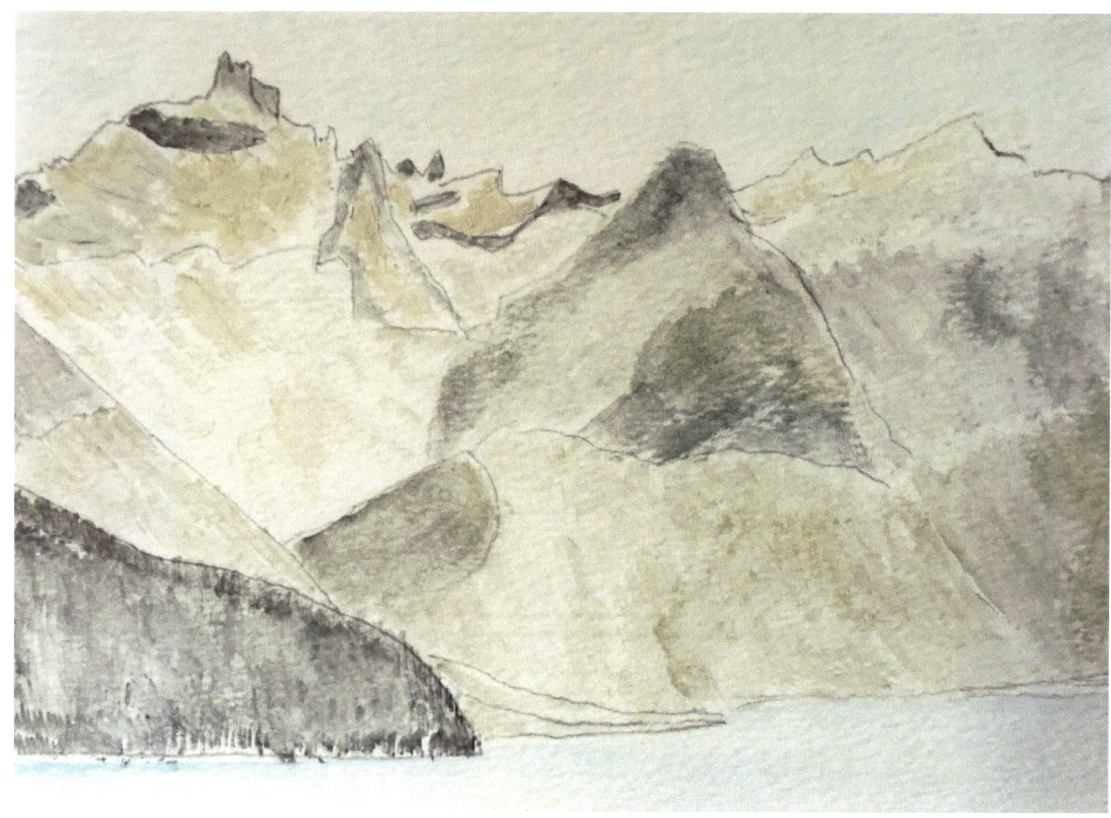

"One thing I've always loved about the mountains – the quiet."

Como Peaks

© 2019 by Craig Michael Maki

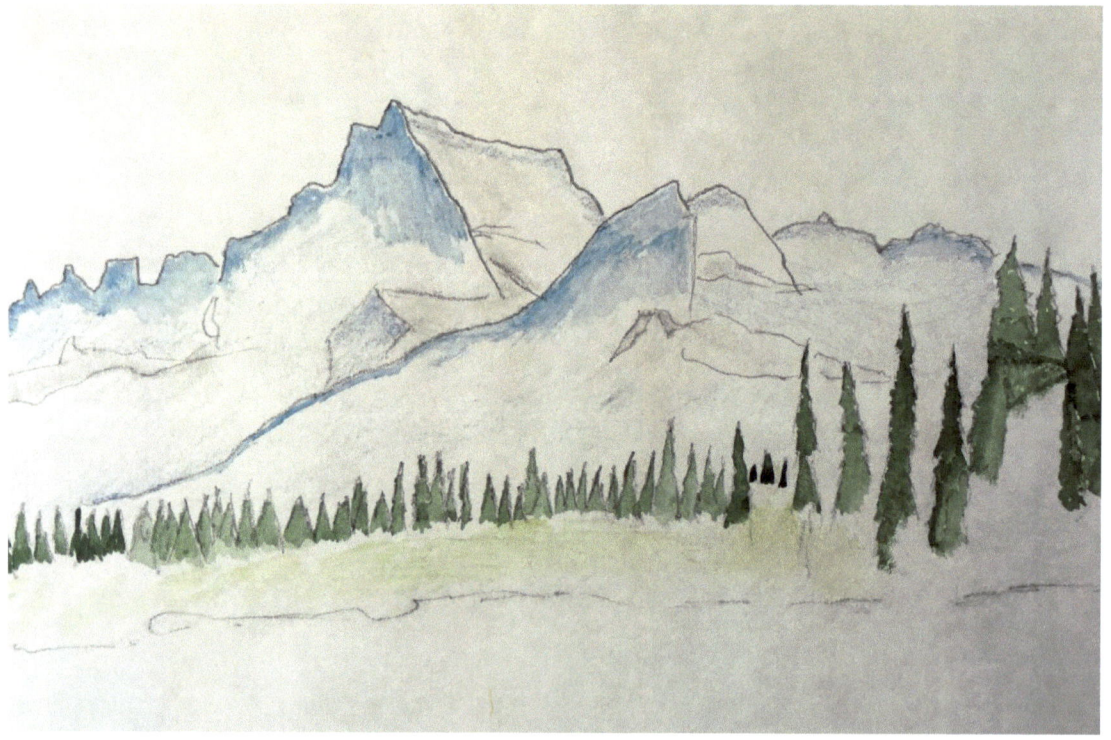

"Glacier Park is called the Crown of the Continent."

Swiftcurrent Lake

© 2019 by Craig Michael Maki

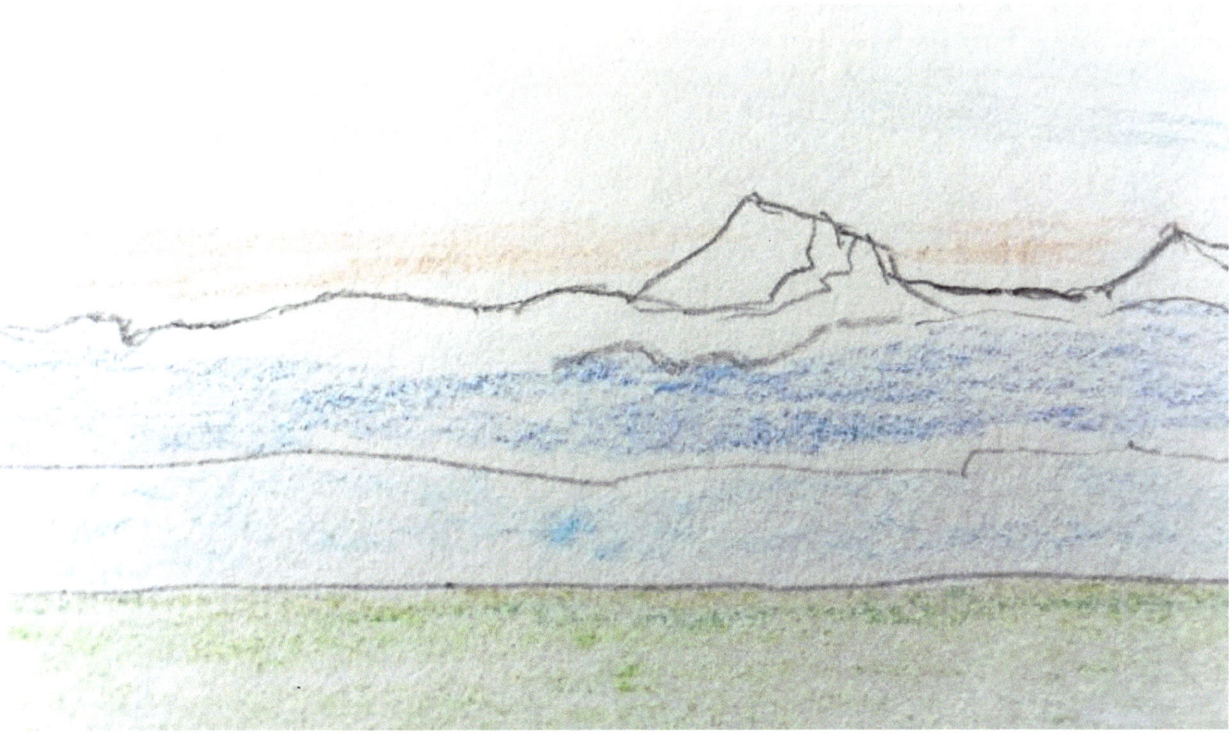

Mountain Pigments © 2019 by Craig Michael Maki

"The various hues and pigments of the distant mountain peaks are as varied as the shapes they form."

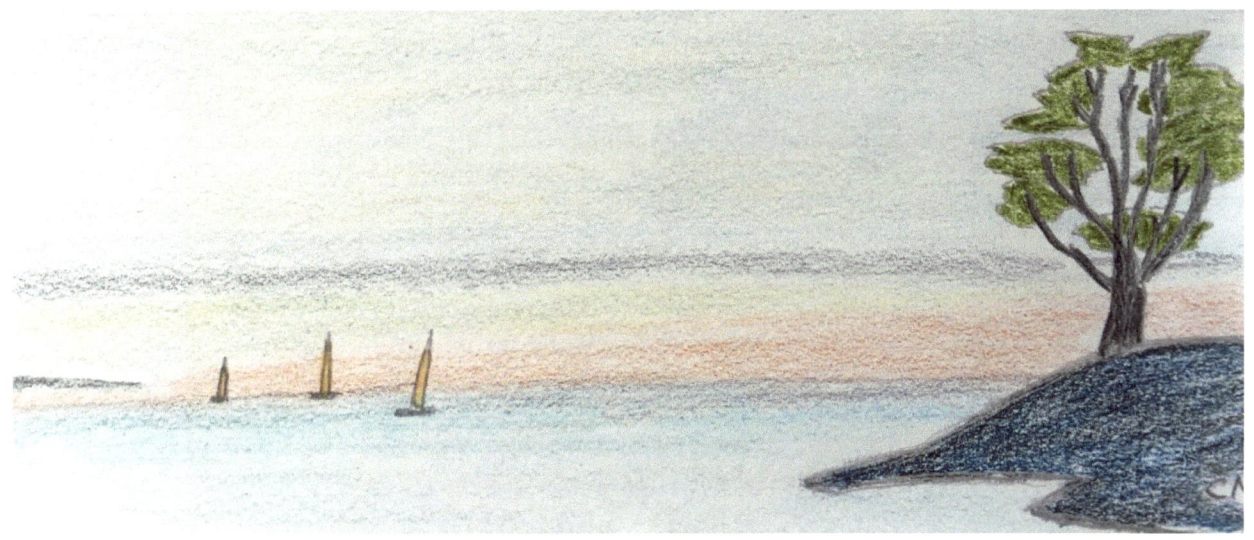

Sunset Rock © 2019 by Craig Michael Maki

"There is something special about a sunset, especially with smooth waters and sailboats on the horizon."

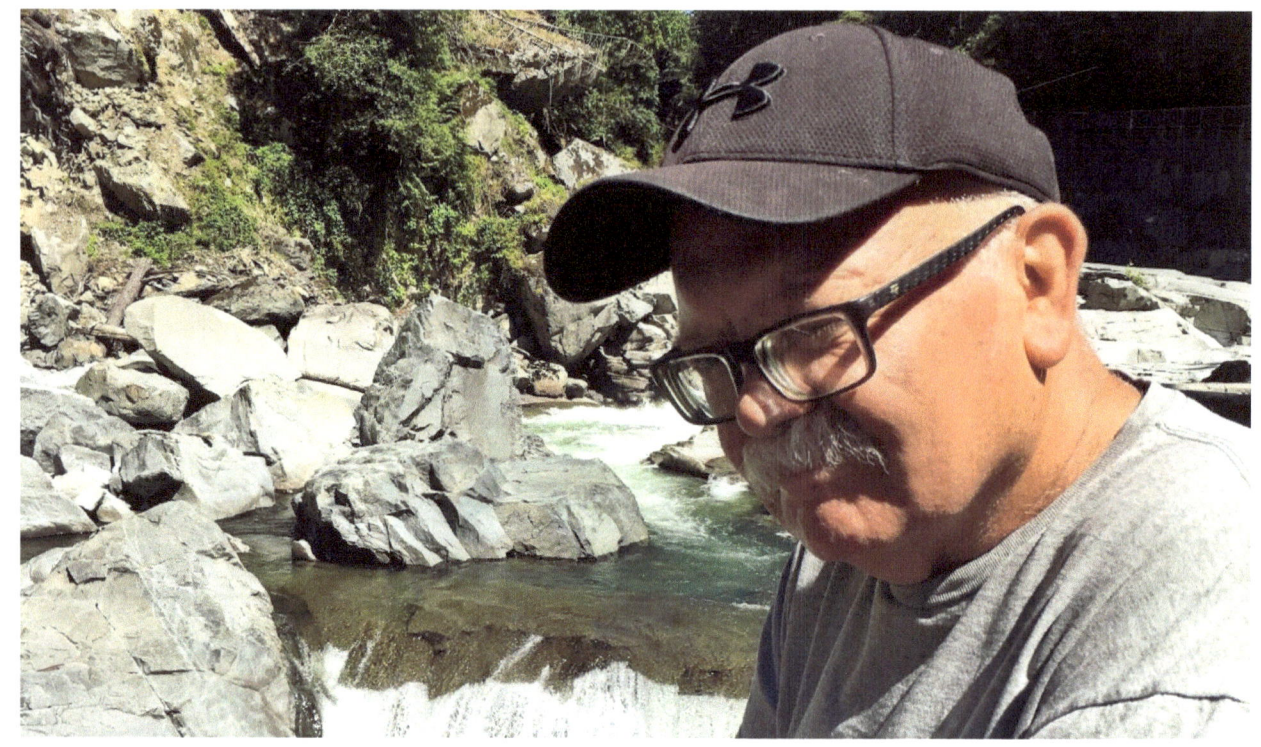

About The Artist

A native of Butte, Montana, Craig Michael Maki has been sketching and painting all of his life. With an intense enthusiasm for nature and the great outdoors, Craig spends a good portion of his spare time hiking mountain trails, peddling his bicycle, and fishing the blue ribbon streams of Montana. Growing up around old mines and mills, Craig has always had an affinity for old buildings and gallows frames.

Craig's art style is a blend of realism and impressionism. In fact, every time he sits down to create a work he's not sure whether it will lean toward the impressionistic, abstract, or the realistic side. Sometimes Craig's art is a study of contrasts, shapes and outlines. Other times color takes precedence. And then at times he creates the rudimentary essence of a subject and shaves it down to the basics.

Craig likes to escape from his worries and concerns with his creative process, and that's why he doesn't like to follow any set structure. His subject matter varies widely and includes wildlife, historical buildings and ghost towns, and country landscapes. He likes to add a touch of realism to the animals and fish he draws. He loves to let color take the helm in his landscapes. And he uses delineating line work as a trademark of his historic pieces. As Craig states, "When sketching or painting something that actually exists, I like to study the subject matter -- including color, shape, contrast and overall layout. On the other hand sometimes I just sit down and create something from my memory or imagination. In that case I kind of let the art take me where it wants to go. I guess that is why my art is so varied."

Everything that Craig creates brings intense joy to his day. Therefore it is his sincere hope that others may experience at least a bit of that enjoyment as they view his artwork.

www.ingramcontent.com/pod-product-compliance
Lightning Source LLC
Chambersburg PA
CBHW040415220526
45473CB00004B/1244